THE GROUND OF GOOD THEOLOGY

The Ground *of* Good Theology

A Beginner's Guide *for* *the* Faithful Study of God

DALE PARTRIDGE

Relearn Press

SEDONA, ARIZONA

Published in Sedona, Arizona by Relearn.org
Written by Dale Partridge
First Edition / First Printing
Cover Image: Painting: "Llyn Ogwen From the South" Water-color by George Fennel Robson 1790-1833 in the Ante Room at Penrhyn Castle.
Sourced through Alamy.
Printed in the U.S.A.

Relearn Press is a companion ministry of Relearn.org. For information, please contact us through our website at Relearn.org.

To my Seminary professors Dr. Steven Lawson, Dr. Brad Klassen, Dr. Brian Biedebach, Dr. James White, and Dr. Jeffrey Johnson who each took the time to guide my journey in studying God.

Our Ministry

The mission of Relearn.org is simple:
Bring the church back to the Bible.
This is the driving force behind each of our
books, digital products, and podcasts.

Our Companion Ministries

ReformationSeminary.com
ReformationFellowship.org
MailTheGospel.org
StandInVictory.org
UltimateMarriage.com

Table *of* Contents

Chapter Zero

THE GROUND OF THEOLOGICAL HEALTH

THE GROUND OF THEOLOGICAL HEALTH

In 2017, I became ill. At first, my symptom list was short and manageable including low body temperature, stomach pain, and dizziness. Months later, I began experiencing muscle twitches, heart palpitations, and kidney stones. By 2019, I added several more symptoms, including gastritis, insomnia, skin cancer, and air hunger. In February 2021, I had my first seizure and weeks later found blood in my bowels.

Early in my journey, I chased individual symptoms. If my stomach hurt, I assumed it was food. If I had insomnia, I assumed it was stress. In other words, I compartmentalized my approach to treatment. However, after further biological and physiological study, I have realized the body is much more complex and interconnected. Namely, the body is not only parts, but as a whole. That is, the stomach is not simply connected to food but also to hormones. Palpitations are not only driven by heart dysfunction but also by blood thickness. Seizures were not only related to the nervous system but also to histamine release. After this understanding, I began to see the human body as an interdependent set of systems that, when working perfectly together, produce a biological masterpiece. In fact, through it all, I gained clarity and appreciation of God's anatomical and biological design for human health. But more than that, I began to see the ground of my body's dysfunction and how my previous approach was unfruitful.

Now, I promise you this book is not about biology. Having said that, I ask that you continue to bear with me as I believe the lessons learned in biology will be quite instructive in the lessons we must learn regarding theology. That is, these two systems have far-reaching similarities and our process to achieve biological health provides a phenomenal parallel to the process of achieving theological health.

As for my body, it was clear that I was not dealing with acute illness but was experiencing chronic illness from a multiple system attack. The solution was not to partition each system off but to understand each system and its relationship with the other systems of the body. Even more, I needed to understand the means by which those systems produced harmony—or in biological terms, health—to the body as a whole. For that reason, I began my journey by both zooming out and zooming in. If I could compare myself to a tree, I needed to see the whole—the branches, the leaves, and the fruit, but I also needed to see the parts—primarily the roots but also the trunk and the bark. In fact, this cycle of broad and narrow would become the pattern that brought about the most systematic clarity for my journey toward healing.

First, I zoomed out. I needed to understand what "health" was and how this health was achieved. Was health simply the physical feeling of wellness? Not really, because even some cancer patients feel great (until they don't). So what is "health"? In short, it is the body's biological systems working properly to sustain physical integrity. But how was this health achieved? For that, I needed to zoom in. I learned that health began at the cellular level (or in my tree analogy—the roots). If the cells were dysfunctional everything else followed in step. Next, I looked at macro systems and anatomy and then back to micro-systems and molecular biology. So there I was, zooming out and zooming in, looking at the pieces and then the whole, understanding the divisions, subdivisions, and their cooperation. From this approach to biology, and by God's grace, I began to see my malady and restore my body's physical health. That is, my body's systems began to work properly to sustain life.

Unfortunately, bad theology is not as kind as bad health. Let me explain. Bad health has a way of letting you know that something is wrong. Bad theology, however, is not so considerate. That is, most people don't know they're theologically sick. Therefore, we must learn the ground of good theology and how to achieve theological health. That is the premise of this book. But before we move on, let's zoom out.

Chapter One

WHAT IS
THEOLOGY?

———

WHAT IS THEOLOGY?

The word is made up of a distinct prefix and suffix. The suffix *(ology)* is familiar to most as it is seen at the end of many other words in the discipline of academic study. "Ology" is derived from the Greek word *logos* and it means word, idea, concept or logic.

For example, if we put the prefix "bio," which means origin or life, in front of "ology," we end up with the word "biology," which is the idea or concept, or logic of life. Now, the prefix "*Theos*" is the Greek word for God. Therefore, theology is the concept or logic of God Himself. To a modern audience, it's best translated as "the study of God." This study, however, must not be confused with the study of religion. Religion is man's sociological and ritualized response to spiritual apprehensions. That is, it's the study of man's response to spiritual matters rather than the study of God Himself. So when we do theology, we look not to man but to God.

But the scope of God must also be clarified. For example, while the Muslims call the study of Allah *Tahwid*, the word can also be referred to as *theology*. Therefore, we must clarify the means by which we are defining God. As Christians, we hold to the Holy Scriptures (the 66 books of the Bible) as the sole source of our theology. But our clarification must go even further. When we speak of theology as an intellectual discipline within the Christian church, it goes far beyond the study of God as the first person of the Trinity (a.k.a. Theology Proper). Theology is the study of *all* things revealed of God in Holy Scripture. Systematically speaking, this has included a total of ten sub-studies including Angelology (the study of angels), bibliology (the study of the Bible), Christology (the study of Christ), ecclesiology (the study of the church), eschatology (the study of the end times), hamartiology (the study of sin), pneumatology (the study of the Holy Spirit), soteriology (the study of salvation), anthropology (the study of the nature of humanity), and theology proper (the study of the character of God). In a sense, systematic theology (which we will discuss later) is much like anatomy. That is, it is the breaking down of the total system into anatomical parts.

However, since we're talking about God and not the human body we must realize that the study of God is the study which determines the proper study of all other studies. We must think this way because theology demands us to. Theology is permeating because God is permeating. In fact, Colossians 1:15–20 states the following of Jesus Christ—God in flesh:

> "The Son is the image of the invisible God, the firstborn over *all* creation. For in him *all* things were created: things in heaven and on earth, visible and invisible, whether

thrones or powers or rulers or authorities; *all* things have been created through Him and for Him. He is before *all* things, and in Him *all* things hold together. And He is the head of the body, the church; He is the beginning and the firstborn from among the dead, so that in everything he might have the supremacy. For God was pleased to have *all* His fullness dwell in Him, and through Him to reconcile to Himself *all* things, whether things on earth or things in heaven, by making peace through his blood, shed on the cross (emphasis added)."

Romans 11:36 sums this passage up in one sentence, "For from Him and through Him and to Him are *all* things" (emphasis added). Consequently, this places all things under the dominion of theology. We cannot rightly do ethics or engineering or law without theology. We cannot rightly do medicine or art or justice without theology. We cannot rightly do math or science or grammar without theology. James Nickel, the author of *Mathematics: Is God Silent?* writes, "The biblical God had designed the universe in a rational and orderly fashion; in fact, so orderly that it could be described mathematically."[1] Therefore Christian theology, in one sense, is the lens by which we see all other things. It eliminates neutrality. There is no thing that can be detached from God. Theology, done right, is invasive and dominating. It colors everything from what we see and how we think, to how

---

1 James Nickel, *Mathematics: Is God Silent?* (Vallecito, Calif.: Ross House Books, 2001).

we feel and what we do in every area of our lives.

Producing Healthy Theology

While biological health is defined as the body's biological systems working properly together to sustain physical integrity, theological health is our theological systems working properly together to maintain doctrinal integrity. Dr. Scott Swain of Reformed Theological Seminary spoke in similar terms when he wrote, "Doctrine is among the things that matter most for the well-being of the Christian and the church. Sound, or "healthy," doctrine provides a pattern that, when followed, promotes healthy faith and love."[2] Essentially, our approach to good health is similar to our approach to good theology. However, in theology, the means to achieve health is not food, exercise and vitamins but truth, Scripture, and doctrine. Our aim isn't to achieve biological wellness but theological soundness. Our labor isn't to comprehend gastrointestinal or circulatory relationships but soteriological and anthropological relationships. Our fight is to find the ground of theological health. In short, we want to arrive at theological integrity and fortitude. That is, we want correct thinking about God. We want to arrive at coherent, congruent, and uncontaminated truth about the Maker and Ruler of this world. Because when we see God rightly, all other things are seen clearly. John MacArthur once said, "Doctrine matters. What you believe about God, the gospel, the nature of

2 R.C. Sproul, *What Is Sound Doctrine?*, Ligonier Ministries, accessed June 15, 2022, https://www.ligonier.org/learn/articles/what-sound-doctrine/.

man, and every major truth addressed in Scripture filters down to every area of your life. You and I will never rise above our view of God and our understanding of His Word."[3]

Theological health, however, is both difficult to achieve and to maintain. We dwell in a fallen body with sinful desires, and we live in a hostile environment filled with lies, sensationalism, and false teaching. The same is true in biology. We live in a fallen body that is susceptible to disease, sickness, and injury. We also live in a world with a thousand untested solutions, hollow supplements, and bad doctors. In fact, if you haven't noticed, more and more people are chronically ill. More people have food allergies and autoimmune diseases than ever before. More people are becoming mysteriously unwell. To that end, the question I have yet to answer for you is, "What was making *me* so sick?" Namely, what was the root cause of my list of debilitating symptoms? What was preventing me from maintaining biological health? The answer, I believe, will be both fascinating and edifying as I connect it to my theological comparison.

After years of investigation, it turns out I had black mold poisoning from a previous building where I had lived or worked. After spending thousands of hours in a water-damaged structure, festering mycotoxins had infiltrated my biological system and were slowly killing me. Mold spores invaded my body through my lungs and hit my bloodstream. The primary objective of mycotoxins is to impair the immune system that attacks them. With enough exposure, these toxins succeed in their suppression efforts and,

---

3 John MacArthur, "Grace to You," Newsletter from Aug. 14, 2007.

as a result, cause a variety of biological systems to falter. Allergic reactions begin, inflammation erupts, and autoimmunity takes root. This is why my symptoms seemed so disconnected and sporadic. I wasn't dealing with one acute issue but a systemic issue causing multiple system collapse. Additionally, mold assaults the liver, and its ability to filter toxins is significantly reduced. As a result, the body becomes more and more toxic and susceptible to pathogens, infections, viruses, and parasites. Mold toxicity, in my opinion, tops the list of most dangerous threats to human biology because any disease that attacks the ability to fight off other diseases is the most concerning disease.

Interestingly, in an interview with my friend Johnny Ardavanis, John MacArthur brilliantly connects this biological reality to an instructive theological lesson for both Christians and the local church:

> "What is the greatest physical danger in the human body? I would say a deficient immune system, because then you could die of a hundred diseases. In the church it's the same thing—a deficient immune system—which is the inability to discern truth from error—it's not recognizing deception. Anything that is not true has potential to do severe damage to the church and there are a hundred heresies that can kill a church."[4]

---

4 Jonny Ardavanis, "John MacArthur Ep. 6," Spotify (Jonny Ardavanis, n.d.), accessed June 15, 2022, https://open.spotify.com/show/3zRD4xDc5spuY1NVeL-wVY0?si=a7cb3a0de3704406.

The similarities between biology immunity and theology immunity are great. Both are systematically arranged. Both require good roots to produce good fruit. Both are at severe risk when they cannot identify systemic errors or hazards. Both need to be proactive to keep their immune systems healthy. Both need to be vigilant against threats. Both need to aggressively pursue the source of their health.

Like biological health, theological health is not easy to achieve—especially if you're already sick—namely, if your view of God has been perverted or distorted by false religion or heresies. Maybe you come from Mormonism or Roman Catholicism and you can't grasp the grace of God. Maybe you come from Islam and you only see Christ as a prophet and not the Messiah. Maybe you come from a Church of Christ or Jehovah's Witness community where you must justify yourself by works and not by faith alone. Whatever religious damage has been done, can be healed. To turn the tide, find sound doctrine, and heal your theology you must immediately face three complex and pressing questions: 1) What is truth? 2) Who is the God of truth? and 3) Where can truth be found? These three questions are shackled to one another—like three sides of a pyramid. You cannot have truth if you cannot define truth. You cannot define truth if you cannot find truth. You cannot find truth if you do not know the God of truth. We will confront these three matters in the following chapters. Together, we will see their inseparable oneness. We will see how truth, Scripture, and God are, in reality, various expressions of the same Being. Ultimately, we will see how they form the ground of good theology. But more than that, we will see how we can build upon that ground with faithful doctrine that will enable us to construct a healthy systematic theology—that is, a multi-faceted and cohesive compression of God that leads us not only to theological health but also to rightful doxology.

Chapter Two

WHAT IS
TRUTH?

———

WHAT IS TRUTH?

A young girl once walked into her grandfather's library full of old books, leather couches, and a beautiful grand piano. Her grandfather was a master pianist who had perfect pitch and could identify musical notes by ear.

She had recently begun taking singing lessons earlier that week and said, "Papa, I learned to sing a C note today." She stood proper and belted out the note and then looked up to her grandfather. The old man replied, "No, sweetie, that was not C." He then walked to a tuning fork in the corner of the room and struck it "That's C." As the note radiated throughout the library he said, "That is C. It is C today. It was C five thousand years ago, and it will be C five thousand years from today." The girl said, "But my note sounded so good." The grandfather said, "It does not matter if it sounds good, feels good, or even works with your song, it is not C and it never will be C. However, if you let me help you tune your ear to C, it will become the basis and cornerstone for all other musical notes. But, sweetie, if you get C wrong, your other notes will never be right. C is the first link in an entire system of sound. In fact, it's the only system that can produce music."

Like music, truth is bound to reality. We may say something like "all sound is music" but that does not correspond to reality. "Music" is simply a word to describe a defined system of sound. Whether we like it or dislike it, melody and harmony can only be made with specific sounds (or musical notes). We have classified these sounds (A, B, C, D, E, F, and G) but we have not defined them. Reality has defined them. We cannot change reality. That is, we cannot change the vibration frequencies of physics. They are what they are. In the same way, we may say "all truth is relative" but that does not correspond to reality, either. Truth is not relative. For example, if I meet someone who says, "Dale, you believe Jesus was God and that's good for you because you believe it's true. But it's not true for me. So do not make *your* truth *my* truth," this is a classic expression of relativism. However, this person doesn't understand that truth cannot be relative. Namely, Jesus is either God or He is not. Jesus cannot be God for me and not God for Him. If He is God, He is God for everybody. If He is not God, then He is not God for anybody. Let me offer another example. If I say, "Boiling water will burn your skin" nobody will say, "Dale, that's good for you because you believe it's true. But it's not true for me." They won't say that because they know this claim is objective and not subjective. If boiling water will burn my human skin, it will burn all people's skin (including theirs). The effect of the boiling water on human skin does not change if we deny the effect. That is to say, boiling water burns human skin whether we believe it to be true or not. Therefore, there is no *my* truth and *your* truth. There is just truth. In fact, to claim "there is no objective truth" is a self-defeating claim. That is, in order for that claim to be objectively true, there would need to be objective truth. But that claim states there is no objective truth making it a self-refuting claim. So, what is really going on? It's actually quite simple; people only embrace relativism when it threatens their personal desires. Namely, relativism is a form of escapism. It's a convenient copout. It's man's attempt to explain away absolutes when those absolutes endanger his desire to sin.

The failure of relativism is most painfully exposed when it pertains to morality. That is, the identification of what is right and wrong. The question immediately becomes, "Is there objective right and wrong? If so, who determines the actions?" In other words, who has the power to declare it's not right for you to murder or sleep with another person's spouse, or to rob a bank, or to vandalize your neighbor's house? Ultimately, who gets to tell you that you've committed wrong and must pay the consequences? In other words, if you agree there is evil in the world (e.g., rape, murder, deception, kidnapping, human trafficking, etc.), then you must assume there's also good in the world (e.g., love, joy, peace, patience, kindness, gratitude, faithfulness, gentleness, and self-control). However, when you assume there is objective good and evil, you assume there is such a thing as an objective moral law by which you can rightly differentiate what is good from what is evil. But if you assume there is an objective moral law, you must also assume an objective Moral Law Giver.

That is, objectivity cannot be produced by man because it would be subjective. Objectivity must flow from something above and beyond man—something transcendent and something with the authority to impose this objective moral law upon us. To state it plainly, if morality exists it cannot be subjective. That is, we do not each make up our own morals, whether individually or corporately (e.g., as a city, religion, country, etc.). If this was the case, we must agree there is no objective Moral Law Giver, which means there is no objective moral law. If there is no objective moral law, there is no objective good. If there is no objective good, there is no objective evil, and, as a result, we end up in a world by which one person (or community) can hurt another person (or community) according to their morals, and nobody has any valid grounds to define it as wrong. If this is the case, we cannot be outraged by suicide bombers, human sacrifice, kidnapping, or the Holocaust. For if there is no objective moral law by which we can condemn such acts for being objectively evil or punishable, then we have no universal, everlasting, and just grounds to claim any act is morally right or wrong. It was Adolf Hitler who famously said, "I have freed Germany from the stupid and degrading fallacies of conscience and morality... We will train young people before whom the world will tremble."[5] He was correct. He trained men who had no objective view of morality and, as a result, could suppress the guilt and shame for committing atrocious actions. Relativism, in morality or

5 Carol-Ann Hooper and Una McCluskey, *Psychodynamic Perspectives on Abuse: The Cost of Fear* (London: Jessica Kingsley Publishers, 2000).

otherwise, is an unlivable way to operate. It leads to utter chaos and death. Michael Novak in his famous essay *Awakening from Nihilism* writes:

"Relativism is an invisible gas, odorless, deadly, that is now polluting every free society on earth. It is a gas that attacks the central nervous system of moral striving. 'There is no such thing as truth,' they teach even the little ones. 'Truth is bondage. Believe what seems right to you. There are many truths as there are (many) individuals. Follow your feelings. Do as you please. Get in touch with yourself.' Those who speak in this way prepare the jail of the twenty-first century."[6]

It quickly becomes obvious that evil does exist, that we do have an objective Moral Law and there must be an objective Moral Law Giver. In fact, the book of Romans confirms that even those who have not heard of God's objective Moral Law (The Ten Commandments) have been given the substance of this Moral Law in their inner being. It reads, "For when Gentiles, who do not have the law, by nature do what the law requires, they are a law to themselves, even though they do not have the law. They show that the work of the law is *written on their hearts*, while their conscience also bears witness, and their conflicting thoughts accuse or even excuse them" (Rom. 2:14–15; emphasis added).

---

6 Michael Novak, *Awakening from Nihilism: Why Truth Matters* (London: IEA Health and Welfare Unit, 1995).

The title of this chapter is *What Is Truth?* I believe you expect an answer to that question. Philosophy and metaphysics answers this question with what is called the *correspondence theory of truth*. The theory states that truth or falsity of a statement is determined only by how it relates to the world and whether it accurately describes (i.e., corresponds with) that world.[7] In short, truth is that which corresponds to reality. If someone says, "The woman held a gun." There must be, in reality, a woman, a gun, and a physical relationship between the woman and the gun. The problem, however, arises when there is a disagreement with what reality is. As we know, we live in a fallen world where people struggle to define things like "woman." As a result, determining if a "woman" truly held a gun, becomes more complex. Having said that, when we operate under the premise that we have an objective Moral Law Giver who can provide objective reality, objective definitions are not difficult. That is, our subjective perspective of reality and our emotions or preferences do not determine reality, God does. The Creator defines His creation. Ultimately, God defines truth. My preaching professor during my time at The Master's Seminary, Dr. Steven Lawson, said, "Theologically, truth is that which is consistent with the mind, will, character, glory, and being of God."[8] Namely, truth is that which corresponds to the revelation and instruction of God.

---

7 "Correspondence Theory of Truth," Wikipedia (Wikimedia Foundation, May 23, 2022), last modified May 23, 2022, accessed June 15, 2022, https://en.m.wikipedia.org/wiki/Correspondence_theory_of_truth.

8 Steven Lawson, "What Is Truth? ," Ligonier Ministries, accessed June 15, 2022, https://www.ligonier.org/learn/articles/what-is-truth.

Now while I have attempted to address our first question "What is truth?" Two of our three interconnected questions remain. The second is "Who is the God of truth?" and the third is, "Where can truth be found." Because of the interwoven nature of these two remaining matters, it was actually quite difficult for me to choose the appropriate chapter order. Augustine famously said, "Where I found truth, there I found my God, who is the truth itself."[9] As you will see, knowing there is a God and finding His revelation of reality are really two sides of the same coin. God, and His revelation, are completely and utterly unified. There are no shadows or contradictions. There is no way to isolate these matters. Having said that, to understand the dimensions of both God and truth, I believe confronting the issue of God first appears to be most fruitful.

---

9 Augustine and Henry Bettenson, The City of God (London, England: Penguin Books, 2003).

Chapter Three

WHO IS THE GOD
OF TRUTH?

———

WHO IS THE GOD OF TRUTH?

Proverbs 19:2 says, "It is not good for a soul to be without knowledge…" That is to say, a soul without comprehension of identity, location, direction, or purpose is lost. In short, ignorance is *not* bliss when it comes to the soul.

As a result, humans look only to what they know—self. They seek self-fulfillment, self-satisfaction, and self-aggrandizement. They read self-help books to become more self-confident and elevate their self-esteem. Their ultimate goal is to self-actualize through self-expression culminating in self-image. Their ultimate response is self-love where they continue to seek self-pleasure as their central expression of self-worship.

Human beings are made to worship. Plutarch, a first-century Greek philosopher once said, "If we traverse the world it is possible to find cities without walls, without letters, without kings, without coin, without schools and theaters; but a city without a temple, or that practiceth not worship, prayer, and the like, no one ever saw."[10] In other words, it is undeniable; worship is ingrained into

---

10 Charles Octavius Boothe, Plain Theology for Plain People (S.l.: Albatros Publishers, 2020).

human design. We are worshippers because there is something or someone who is to be worshiped. C. S. Lewis says:

"Creatures are not born with desires unless satisfaction for those desires exists. A baby feels hunger: well, there is such a thing as food. A duckling wants to swim: well, there is such a thing as water. Men feel sexual desire: well, there is such a thing as sex. If I find in myself a desire which no experience in this world can satisfy, the most probable explanation is that I was made for another world."[11]

Mr. Lewis is making the point that natural desire implies the reality of natural fulfillment. We worship because we desire to worship. We desire to worship because God fashioned within us this desire at creation. However, the soul without identity, location, direction, or purpose will always arrive at misdirected worship; therefore, it's not a matter of *will* we worship, but *what* we will worship.

I live in Sedona, Arizona. It's a small town in the Southwest with a population of approximately 10,000 people. However, over 3.5 million people visit our town every year. Why? First and foremost, they come to see the red rock formations that saturate our area. But it's much more than that. Sedona is the New Age capital of the world. People come to Sedona to worship. Thousands of people bow before the rocks, visit geographic locations called vortexes, pay for psychic readings, perform séances with

---

11 C. S. Lewis, Mere Christianity (New York: Harper Collins, 2015), 136–37.

witches, study the paranormal, praise the stars, and gather in synagogues and temples and before shrines. In Sedona, there are few atheists. In fact, it's very much like the account of Paul in the book of Acts as he enters the city of Athens.

"Now while Paul was waiting for them at Athens, his spirit was provoked within him as he saw that the city was full of idols…. So Paul, standing in the midst of the Areopagus, said: "Men of Athens, I perceive that in every way you are very religious. For as I passed along and observed the objects of your worship, I found also an altar with this inscription: 'To the Unknown God.' What therefore you worship as unknown, this I proclaim to you. The God who made the world and everything in it, being Lord of heaven and earth, does not live in temples made by man, nor is he served by human hands, as though he needed anything, since he himself gives to all mankind life and breath and everything" (Acts 17:16, 22–25).

This, in a very real sense, has been a description of my local ministry. I live in a community of misdirected worshippers. As I mentioned, the objects of worship range from rocks and animals to shrines and self. But one thing is clear, the people here passionately seek out spiritual exaltation. The tragedy is that it's an empty exaltation. It's wicked worship. It's both of these things because it's misdirected worship. Like the people of Athens who incorrectly point their praises to "The Unknown God", the people of Sedona lay before stone and self. The truth is, without identity, location, direction, or purpose people are lost. The 19th century theologian, Octavious Boothe once wrote,

"Before the charge 'know thyself,' ought to come the far greater charge, 'know thy God.'"[12] Therefore, the question all persons must confront is not "Who am I?" but "Who is God?"

While the people of Sedona and Athens rarely reject the existence of God altogether, atheists are no small crowd. That is, there are still millions who overlook their intrinsic need to worship, who are blind to the divine evidence of creation, who refuse to see intelligent design, and who hate the notion of a God who demands their obedience. Psalm 14:1 says, "The fool says in his heart, "There is no God." They are corrupt, they do abominable deeds; there is none who does good." To deny God is to deny reason. Nobody looks at a wedding dress and denies the existence of a seamstress. Nobody looks at medieval paintings and denies the painter. Therefore, to look at the fruit tree or the solar system or the human body—which beholds complexity and wisdom far beyond our comprehension—and deny a Maker, is foolishness. History celebrates makers. We applaud the architect and the mason, we hail the author and the artists, but when it comes to the Maker of *all* things, humanity directs its gratitude elsewhere—to "science" or "evolution" or the "universe." Foolishness! The Puritan writer, Stephen Charnock once wrote, "Every plant, every atom, as well as every star, at the first meeting, whispers this in our ears, "I have a Creator; I am witness to a Deity."[13] Namely, it becomes intellectually absurd

---

12 Charles Octavius Boothe, Plain Theology for Plain People (S.l.: Albatros Publishers, 2020).

13 Stephen Charnock, Discourses upon the Existence and Attributes of God

to believe in an un-created world. Evidence, experience, and reason protect us from such lunacy.

For those too reasonable to subscribe to atheism, agnosticism has found a home. This community refuses to deny the existence of God but, instead, advocates for an *unknowable* God. This, as we will see, does not solve humanity's search for objective truth nor direction for the lost soul. If God is unknowable, then truth is unknowable. That is, without a defined God who can offer objective truth through divine revelation, humanity is left to do the defining. Consequently, Mother Earth can be your god, Allah can be your god, Brahma can be your god, or aliens can be your god. In short, agnosticism allows for God to be anything we want it to be. Our imagination becomes the author of our deity. Ultimately, when we get to define God, we place ourselves above God. As one above God, we ultimately become god. This, as you see, supports the thesis of this paragraph: agnosticism is just as foolish as atheism.

However, the admission of a *defined* God becomes the admission of *defined* truth. That is, to identify the Divine is to locate the source of truth. But more than that, it is to define God's character, being, and will. Therefore, while the atheist and the agnostic are content with ambiguity, theological definition becomes essential. However, we are not looking for religious ideas. We are not looking for spiritual insight. We are looking for God, namely, who is the only Creator, Sustainer, and Restorer of all things. Who is holy, righteous, just, and true? Who is

(Grand Rapids: Baker Book House, 1979), 9.

worthy of all glory, praise, and honor? Who is infinite, eternal, infallible, unchangeable, all-knowing, all-powerful, and wholly independent? Who is this one true God? To understand these aspects of God, is to see our responsibility to God. From here, we can attain identity, location, direction, and purpose. From here God becomes our fixed point of reference. He becomes the Ruler by which all things can be measured.

John Calvin likened our view of God to spectacles. He said, and I'm paraphrasing, "Apart from God, we stumble around in the dark. God is necessary to see the world rightly."[14] A. W. Tozer, in his book *The Knowledge of the Holy* said, "What comes into our minds when we think about God is the most important thing about us."[15] Richard Rushdooney once wrote, "How we view God will determine how we view everything."[16] Therefore, the definition of this God cannot be flawed. That is, it cannot be defined by, or delivered from, man. On the contrary, the definition of God must be revealed by God alone to man. The process of divine revelation is the heart of the following chapter. There I will expound upon the two types of revelation taught in Scripture. Now, as it pertains to a definition of God—a definition that meets the standards mentioned above—we must look briefly to the Doctrine of God, the Trinity and more specifically to the

14 John Calvin, Institutes of the Christian Religion (London: James Clarke & Co, 1962).

15 A. W. Tozer, The Knowledge of the Holy: The Attributes of God, Their Meaning in the Christian Life (United States: General Press, 2019).

16 R.J Rushdooney, Systematic Theology (Vallecito, California: Ross House Books, 2000).

incarnate Christ.

Defining God

The Doctrine of God is essentially a definition of God. It's often referred to as *Theology Proper* and focuses its study on God the Father. In short, the Doctrine of God is an organized set of biblically revealed definitions of the attributes of God. It examines God's omnipresence, omniscience, omnipotence, and eternality. It teaches us about who God is and what He does. That is, it attempts to answer the question, "From Genesis to Revelation what does Scripture teach about the character of God?" This doctrine is essential as it lays the foundation for the study of further biblical topics. That is, like the little girl who misdefined C, if you get the Doctrine of God wrong all additional study will be skewed. C. D. Cole in his book *Definitions of Doctrine* brilliantly said, "The man who thinks right about God will not be far wrong in his thinking about other things. A thousand evils grow out of wrong conceptions about God."[17] But more than that, our depth and clarity of the Doctrine of God will directly influence the height and fervency of our worship. Now, in this book, I do not intend to cover the Doctrine of God, my intention is to simply make you aware of its existence, priority, and importance.

Included in the Doctrine of God generally includes reference to the Trinity. Christianity is a monotheistic faith. That is, we believe in one God. Historically, however, this has caused some confusion because the Bible declares God to be three-in-one.

---

17 Greg Wilson, "The Doctrine of God," I, accessed June 15, 2022, https://libcfl. com/articles/cole-1.htm#intro.

In fact, the most succinct definition of the Trinity is: One in essence, three in person. In the Westminster Larger Catechism, the ninth question asks, "How many persons are there in the Godhead?" The answer is likely the most concise I've read. It states, "There are three persons in the Godhead, the Father, the Son, and the Holy Ghost: and these three are one true, eternal God, the same in substance, equal in power and glory; although distinguished by their personal properties."[18] R. C. Sproul brings further Trinitarian clarity when he wrote, "The Christian faith is not polytheistic, confessing many individual gods, each with its own peculiar divine nature. The Christian faith is not unitarian, confessing that the one divine nature is possessed only by a single person or a single acting subject. Instead, the Christian faith says that three distinct persons are the one divine nature in its entirety. The Father possesses all that makes God who He is; the Son possesses all that makes God who He is; and the Spirit possesses all that makes God who He is."[19] Although the doctrine of the Trinity cannot be fully grasped by the human mind, we affirm this doctrine because this is how God reveals Himself to us in Scripture. God is three and God is one. Ultimately, the term "Trinity" (which does not appear anywhere in the Bible) offers us a theological framework to further comprehend God as revealed in Scripture.

18 "The Westminster Larger Catechism," Ligonier Ministries, accessed June 15, 2022, https://www.ligonier.org/learn/articles/westminster-larger-catechism.

19 R.C. Sproul, "One in Essence, Three in Person: Reformed Bible Studies & Devotionals at Ligonier.org: Reformed Bible Studies & Devotionals at Ligonier.org," Ligonier Ministries, accessed June 15, 2022, https://www.ligonier.org/learn/devotionals/one-essence-three-person.

However, the most accessible definition of God for the human mind is not theology written on paper but divinity made flesh. It is in the Person of Jesus Christ that we, as humans, see God most clearly. The Apostle John in his opening remarks of his Gospel wrote, "In the beginning was the Word, and the Word was with God, and the Word was God. He was in the beginning with God. All things came into being through Him, and apart from Him nothing came into being that has come into being" (John 1:1–4). A few verses later he states, "And the Word became flesh, and dwelt among us, and we saw His glory, glory as of the only begotten from the Father, full of grace and truth" (John 1:14). In Scripture, Jesus is referred to as "The Word of God." The word *Word* (Λόγοσ in the Greek or transliterated as "Logos"), as stated earlier in this book, is referring to the logic of God or the mind of God or even the wisdom of God. Namely, it is representative of the being of God. It was by God's Word that all creation came into existence (Gen 1:3, Ps 33:6; 107:20, Prov 8:27) It is by His Word that God brings forth salvation (Rom 10:17). It is by His Word that He makes judgments and produces fruitfulness in His people (Heb 4:12; John 12:48; 15:3; 17:17). Furthermore, in Scripture, the Word of God is referred to as truth. In John 17:17, Jesus prays, "Sanctify them in the truth; Your word is truth." Psalm 119:60 states, "The sum of your word is truth, and every one of your righteous rules endures forever." Essentially, in the incarnation of God—Jesus Christ—truth becomes a Person. It's why Jesus said, "I am the way, and the truth, and the life; no one comes to the Father but through Me" (John 14:6). In short, there is no truth outside of the person of Jesus Christ—He is truth incarnate.

The 14th-century theologian Thomas Kempis in his famous work *The Imitation of Christ* wrote of Jesus's claim, "Follow thou me. I am the way and the truth and the life. Without the way there is no going; without the truth there is no knowing; without the life there is no living. I am the way which thou must follow; the truth which thou must believe; the life for which thou must hope..."[20] Ultimately, Jesus is the Word and the Word is truth. Now, we know God speaks to humanity primarily by His Son (Heb 1:1–2). But is the incarnate Word the only mode of divine communication given to mankind? That is, is Jesus the only means of revelation? If that were the case, then Scripture would have no place. The 16th-century reformer, Thomas Adams reminds us of the relationship between the written Word and the incarnate Word when he writes, "Christ is the sum of the whole Bible, prophesied, typified, prefigured, exhibited, demonstrated, to be found in every leaf, almost in every line, the Scriptures being but as it were the swaddling bands of the child Jesus."[21] Yes, truth is a Person. But truth is also Scripture. In the following chapter, we move from flesh to text. We see where truth can be found, read, and preached.

---

20 Thomas Kempis, The Imitation of Christ (New York: Dorset Press, 1952).

21 The Works of Thomas Adams (1862; reprint, Tanski, 1998), 3:224

Chapter Four

WHERE CAN TRUTH
BE FOUND?

———

WHERE CAN TRUTH BE FOUND?

Humanity is utterly dependent upon God. As I mentioned earlier in this book, without God, we cannot grasp identity, location, direction, or purpose. In short, I agree with R. C. Sproul when he said, "Without God man has no reference point to define himself."[22a]

The question becomes, how does a person come to know God? The most common responses are 1) by reading about God or 2) hearing about God. However, Scripture teaches that humanity's knowledge of God precedes both reading and hearing. Namely, that He is seen in the things that are made. Therefore, we must acknowledge that God is not found; He is revealed. Scripture teaches two primary forms of this divine revelation—general and special. The first deals with the existence of God seen in creation while the second deals with the way of salvation seen in Jesus Christ.

22a R. C. Sproul, Reason to Believe: A Response to Common Objections to Christianity (Grand Rapids, MI: Zondervan Pub. House, 1993).

General Revelation

Article two of the Belgic Confession speaks of general revelation in the following way: "By the creation, preservation, and government of the universe; which is before our eyes as a most elegant book, wherein all creatures, great and small, are as so many characters leading us to see clearly the invisible things of God, even his everlasting power and divinity..."[22] This idea is not philosophical. The footing for this doctrine is most clearly seen in Romans 1:18–23 and most sharply stated in verse 20 which reads, "For since the creation of the world His invisible attributes, His eternal power, and divine nature, have been clearly seen, being understood through what has been made, so that they [the unbelievers] are without excuse." In sum, Paul is declaring that creation (including our very humanity which is made in the image of God (Gen 1:26–27) is sufficient evidence for the existence of God. Ultimately, in creation, humanity is given adequate knowledge of the existence of God leaving the world culpable for their rejection of God. Namely, no person, even those who have never audibly heard of God or seen a Bible, are excused for their atheism. God, through His intelligent design, displayed in the natural world along with the conscience of man (which convicts humanity of their evil deeds) are reasonable witnesses, to condemn them for their rebellion (Rom 2:15–16).

However, while the Bible teaches that humanity knows God (Rom 1:21) it also teaches that humanity denies God (1 Cor

---

22 Nicolaas Hendrik Gootjes, The Belgic Confession: Its History and Sources (Grand Rapids, MI: Baker Academic, 2007).

2:14; 15:34; 1 Thess 4:5; 2 Thess 1:8; 2 Tim 3:7; Titus 1:16; 1 John 4:8). This is best seen in the discipline of classical apologetics. In this approach, apologists aim to intellectually convince others of the existence of God through historical, scientific, and even theological means. Proponents of this approach have wrongly inflated the power of general revelation and incorrectly assessed biblical anthropology. John MacArthur eloquently explains why such a task is futile:

"Is it easy to convince someone that the Bible is the Word of God on the basis of its unity, its scientific, historical accuracy, its miracles, its archaeological evidence? I haven't found that to be the case. In a special series spread over a three-week period I presented such data at a private college in California. I felt the proof was overwhelming and not one person became a believer. Why doesn't it convince all unbelievers when it's so convincing to us? Paul said it when he wrote, 'The man without the Spirit does not accept the things that come from the Spirit of God, for they are foolishness to him and he cannot understand them, because they are spiritually discerned' (1 Cor 2:14)."[23]

The reality is, while general revelation is sufficient for responsibility it is not sufficient for salvation. Namely, creation permits humanity to undoubtedly know God, but not to rightly worship

---

23 John F. MacArthur, "Is the Bible Reliable?," Grace to You, last modified August 18, 2016, accessed June 15, 2022, https://www.gty.org/library/topical-series-library/65/is-the-bible-reliable.

Him. Due to our fallen nature, humanity rejects God even while we see Him. This, of course, is humanity's condemnation and the basis for the doctrine of Total Depravity. Romans 3:10–12 firmly reminds us of the state of the human soul: "There is none righteous, not even one; There is none who understands, There is none who seeks for God; All have turned aside, together they have become useless; There is none who does good, There is not even one."

Now this still doesn't fully answer the question at the opening of this chapter, "How does a person come to know God?" That is to say, if general revelation is not sufficient to persuade a person to know, love, and worship God, how does someone come to a saving knowledge of Jesus Christ? To answer this, we must look to the second form of divine revealing—special revelation.

Special Revelation

Romans 10:17 states, "So faith comes from hearing, and hearing by the word of Christ." That is, there is only one way a person can come to a saving knowledge of God and that is through the *Word of Christ*. Now, this Word of Christ (or revelation of Christ) is received by two (and only two) means: The reading of Scripture and the preaching of Scripture. Paul supports this two-fold structure when, in his letter to the Romans (readable Scripture), he commands the preaching of Scripture. In fact, in all of the New Testament writings, the Apostles share no other means by which the Gospel can take root. In Romans 10:13–14 Paul says, "For "everyone who calls on the name of the Lord will be saved." How then will they call on him in whom they have not believed? And how are they to believe in him of whom they have never heard? And how are they to hear without someone preaching?" Therefore, the river of salvation flows down the two banks of special revelation—reading God's Word or hearing God's Word. Namely, God's Word is the sole vehicle of special revelation. That is to say, the previous and various means of special revelation seen in the Old Covenant such as divine visions, dreams, or other theophanies (e.g., the burning bush [Exod 3:2–3], thunder over Mt. Sanai [Exod 19], and visual revelations [Isa 6:1]) have ceased. These Old Testament forms of special revelation have, in truth, found their fulfillment in the incarnation of Jesus Christ. Namely, Jesus serves as the climactic, ultimate, and final theophany. He is God in the flesh and His Words will never pass away (Mark 13:31). Hebrews 1:1–2 makes this point quite clear, "Long ago, at many times and in many ways, God spoke to our fathers by the prophets, but in these last days he has spoken to us by his Son, whom he appointed the heir of all things, through whom also he created the world." The revelation of Jesus Christ was born in the flesh, recorded in the Gospels, preached in Acts, explained in the epistles, and expected in Revelation and has become, by God's appointment of His Apostles (messengers), the singular and exclusive instrument to bring about saving faith in mankind.

The Doctrine of Scriptural Infallibility

However, the next matter still before us is, if Scripture is the only means of producing a saving knowledge of God, is Scripture infallible and inerrant? More clearly stated, how do we know we can trust the Bible? Wasn't this book put together by men? Are we missing books? How do we know invalid books have not been slipped in? Allow me to approach this issue in two ways. First, we will look at the Bible's internal evidence of infallibility, and second, we will look at its external evidence.

Internal Evidence

The basis for internal evidence is anchored in two verses. The first is 2 Timothy 3:16 where Paul declares, "All Scripture is given by inspiration of God, and is profitable for doctrine, for reproof, for correction, for instruction in righteousness, that the man of God may be complete, thoroughly equipped for every good work." This passage is what many theologians call the kingpin verse for biblical infallibility. The word "all" is a determiner used for emphasis. The implication of this verse is not fuzzy or unclear. It states that *all* Scripture is θεόπνευστος (*theopneustos*) which literally means "God-breathed." Essentially, holy Scripture is God's chosen method by which His words left His mouth for the profit of mankind. And like God who is eternal, His Word is also eternal. In fact, as I mentioned earlier, Jesus Himself says in Matthew 24:35, "Heaven and earth will pass away, but My words will by no means pass away." God's words are not perishable; they are permanent. Their authority, meaning, and command are also permanent.

The second anchoring verse addresses the issue of human involvement. Namely, how can we know that Scripture is the

Word of God and not the word of men? 2 Peter 1:20–21 speaks to this issue when the Apostle writes, "Knowing this first of all, that no prophecy of Scripture comes from someone's own interpretation. For no prophecy was ever produced by the will of man, but men spoke from God as they were carried along by the Holy Spirit." That is, the authoritative element of Scripture—namely the act of speaking for God—does not originate in the mind of man but in the mind and will of God. Furthermore, even the process of revelation from God to man was not dictation, but divine inspiration by which God used the individual gifts and characteristics of His holy men while maintaining the complete integrity of His declarations. James Bannerman summed up the relation between revelation and inspiration when he said, "A supernatural communication of truth from God is a revelation; the supernatural transference of the truth to the written Word is inspiration."[24]

However, in examination of these two passages, the most common challenge from critics becomes an issue of context. For example, their claim is that the passages of 2 Timothy and 2 Peter are speaking only of the inspiration and inerrancy of the Old Testament Scriptures and not the writings of the New Testament. If this is true, then one would assume the Apostles would have rejected their own writings as divinely inspired Scripture and denied any awareness that their Gospels and epistles were the penning of God's eternal words. Therefore, the question becomes: <u>Did the Apostles know that the content they were writing was</u>

24 James Bannerman, Inspiration: The Infallible Truth and Divine Authority of the Holy Scriptures (Edinburgh: T. and T. Clark, 1865),151.

equally holy and divine as the inspired writings of the Old Testament? The answer, I believe is unequivocal and clear—yes, the Apostles recognized their writings as divinely inspired, timeless, and authoritative. We see this in a variety of passages. For example, in 1 Thessalonians 2:13, Paul writes: "For this reason, we also thank God without ceasing, because when you received the Word of God which you heard from us, you welcomed it not as the word of men, but as it is in truth, the Word of God, which also effectively works in you who believe." Eighteenth-Century Baptist theologian John Gill said of this specific passage, "The word delivered by Paul appeared to be agreeable to the Scriptures of Truth, and it bearing His impress and divine authority, they received it with much assurance and certainty, as infallible truth; and which was inviolable to be adhered to, without any alteration, without adding to it or taking from it; and to be had and retained in the greatest esteem and reverence, and never to be departed from: and that they received it in this manner."[25] I agree with Gill's assertion. I believe Paul was fully aware of the spiritual authority of his words by way of preaching as well as by writing. That is, Paul recognized that his commissioned work was divinely supported, endorsed, and sustained. I believe we can see this posture again in this 1 Thessalonians 5:27 when Paul pens, "I charge you by the Lord that this epistle be read to all the holy brethren." Simply put, Paul knew he, as a representative to a king, had the authority to declare spiritual rulings and commands over

25 John Gill, Gill's Commentary (Grand Rapids: Baker Book House, 1980).

God's people.

To look at an even stronger case, let's turn our eyes to 1 Corinthians 14:37 where Paul writes, "If anyone thinks himself to be a prophet or spiritual, let him acknowledge that the things which I write to you are the commandments of the Lord." Here, Paul addresses his own writings as a command of the Lord. In other words, these are not the babblings of a religious leader or the proclamations of a wise man. They are the authorized decrees penned by an official ambassador of the King. To pile on more evidence for this authoritative awareness, the Apostle Peter also affirms this position by acknowledging Paul's writings as Scripture. He writes in 2 Peter 3:14–16, "Therefore, beloved, looking forward to these things, be diligent to be found by Him in peace, without spot and blameless; and consider that the longsuffering of our Lord is salvation—as also our beloved brother Paul, according to the wisdom given to him, has written to you, as also in all his epistles, speaking in them of these things, in which are some things hard to understand, which untaught and unstable people twist to their own destruction, *as they do also the rest of the Scriptures*" (emphasis added).

This theme of divine awareness and scriptural authority continues as Peter maintains this point even about his own writings as he places them at equal status with the Old Testament Scriptures. "Beloved, I now write to you this second epistle (in both of which I stir up your pure minds by way of reminder), that you may be mindful of the words which were spoken before by the holy prophets, and of the commandment of us, the apostles of the Lord and Savior…" (2 Pet 3:1–2). The fact of the matter is this: The human writers of the New Testament knew who the true Author was behind their words. They understood the authority and inerrancy of their writings. But more importantly, this is the evidence of Scripture. I agree with Charles Spurgeon when he said, "If I did not believe in the infallibility of Scripture—the absolute infallibility of it from cover to cover, I would never enter this pulpit again!" If what is in Scripture is merely of men then there is no reason to ever speak of it again. It is mere moralism, religiosity, and empty ideas. But if it is the Word of God—the means of salvation to everyone who believes—then it must be read, studied, and proclaimed.

External Evidence

The Bible exceeds expectations in every category. So while we have immense internal theological and textual evidence to support our trust in the reliability of Scripture, the Bible offers further (and even exceptional) external evidence to bring greater strength to an already compelling case. In physical terms, the Bible is a book made up of 66 shorter books, written by 40 different authors, over a 1500-year period all telling one miraculously unified story ending with the pinnacle Person of Jesus Christ. As it pertains to the New Testament, these books were not collected and made authoritative by the church, the church recognized their authority and collected them based on the universal reception among believers. Sproul once said it this way, "It's one thing to make something authoritative, and it's another thing to recognize something that *already is* authoritative."[26] They recognized the authority of these writings through 1) their author (apostle or direct apostolic representative), 2) their doctrinal alignment with the other received books and the Old Testament, and 3) their overwhelming reception as authoritative Scripture among the early church. The first "canon" or finalized list of New Testament books was the Muratorian Canon, which was compiled in AD 170 (about 70 years after the death of the Apostle John). The Muratorian Canon included all of the New Testament books except Hebrews, James, 1 and 2 Peter, and 3 John. This is not shocking as it took many years to transcribe these letters (by hand), circulate them, and offer time for the church to discern their status. In 393 AD the Council of Hippo and the Council of Carthage (just four years later) affirmed all 27 books of our current New Testament as authoritative. There has never been a church council that disagrees with this conclusion.[27]

In continuing our discussion revolving around external evidence, let's look back at the issue of truth. As I explained in an earlier chapter, truth can be measured. If something is true it will align with reality. That is, if something is true, we see confirmations, accuracies, reason, and harmonies. Ultimately, things line up. On the other hand, if something is false, we see contradictions,

26 R.C. Sproul, The R.C. Sproul Collection Volume 2: Essential Truths of the Christian Faith (Carol Stream, IL: Tyndale House Publishers, 2017).

27 The Journey from Texts to Translations by Paul D. Wegner (Baker Books) offers several helpful chapters that explore this issue with scientific, academic, and historical rigor. Chapter nine which is titled "Canonization of the New Testament presents compelling evidence for New Testament integrity.

conflicts, clashes, and failures. Namely, things don't line up. Over the past 2,000 years, even with the mass accumulation of human knowledge, nothing has been able to disprove the reliability of Scripture. In fact, history continues to produce overwhelming alignment and support for it. For example, more and more secular scientists have acknowledged something cannot come from nothing.[28] That is, they have recognized the universe has a Creator and that matter cannot self-produce. In addition, the flood of Genesis 6–9 has found staggering geological support in recent decades.[29] Furthermore, the cosmic claims of Scripture regarding the shape of the earth, the age of the earth, the evaporative water systems, the biological and physiological claims, and even the solar system have only found further support in modern science. Likewise, archeology and history have shown significant and compelling alignment—from ancient Middle Eastern geography and excavations to consistencies between Scripture and secular historical events. Additionally, the theological and anthropological claims harmonize with humanity more than any other religious writing. Namely, the biblical narrative offers the irrefutable answers to life's most difficult questions. The diagnostic claims regarding the

28 Lee Billings, "Atheism Is Inconsistent with the Scientific Method, Prize-winning Physicist Says," Scientific American (Scientific American, March 20, 2019), last modified March 20, 2019, accessed June 15, 2022, https://www.scientificamerican.com/article/atheism-is-inconsistent-with-the-scientific-method-prizewinning-physicist-says/.

29 Smithsonian Magazine, "Evidence for a Flood," Smithsonian.com (Smithsonian Institution, April 1, 2000), last modified April 1, 2000, accessed June 15, 2022, https://www.smithsonianmag.com/science-nature/evidence-for-a-flood-102813115/.

moral state of mankind, the solution to our spiritual pain, and the future of the church have shown to be profoundly accurate. Put differently, Scripture at work in the human life and heart produces fruitfulness. Nobody can deny the unarguable quality of life available to those who truly follow the Bible. From healthy marriages and loving families to men and women living with integrity. In other words, divorce, adultery, racism, human trafficking, crime, drugs, and addiction are all a result of people who have chosen *not* to follow the instruction of the Bible. As for the prophetic, hundreds of Old Testament and New Testament prophecies have been fulfilled. From Daniel's precise predictions of the rise and fall of four empires from Babylon to Medo-Persia to Greece and Rome, to Isaiah's detailed foretelling of Christ's crucifixion, and even Jesus's prophecy of the destruction of Jerusalem in 70 AD (Matt 24:1–31). Ultimately, the Bible has continued to accurately predict the future. Finally, and one of the more compelling pieces of external evidence is the Bible's adoption as authoritative truth by billions of sober-minded men and women of world history. From kings, emperors, philosophers and scientists to the average mother, carpenter, and child, the Bible is the world's bestselling book. Conservative estimates state over three billion copies are in print and this doesn't count the growing digital consumption of Scripture. In 2021, YouVersion celebrated record Bible engagement worldwide as its Bible App became the first faith-based app to reach 500 million installs. In 2021, approximately 64 billion Bible chapters were read or listened to, which was up

21% compared to 2020 and up 56% compared to 2019.[30] In other words, the Bible's influence is not diminishing. In fact, printing and translation work has been magnified in recent centuries and has no indication of slowing down. While many have attempted to remove it from society, it continues to abide. Billy Graham famously said, "It has been ridiculed, burned, refuted, destroyed, but it lives on. The Bible is the anvil that has worn out many hammers."[31] In short, the Bible offers abundant and substantial external evidence that aligns not only with history, but also with the physical, emotional, moral, and spiritual state of human reality.

But most of all, as a Christian, we can believe in the Bible because Jesus believed in the Bible. Throughout all four Gospels, you can't deny that Jesus took the Scriptures to be historical fact. As Christians, we must ask ourselves if we're willing to believe in Jesus but not Jesus's position on Scripture? During His three-year ministry, He quoted or referenced 78 different verses from 16 different Old Testament books. He calls these references "The Scriptures,""The Word of God," and "The Wisdom of God." Jesus followed the Law of Scripture, fulfilled the prophecy of Scripture, and upheld the integrity of Scripture.

Ultimately, when you read the Bible, there's a distinct supernatural presence. The unity and cohesion are flat-out miraculous.

---

30 Richard D. Hunt, "Bible Interest Not in Decline: Youversion Bible App Hits an Incredible Half-Billion Free Downloads," LOVE, accessed June 15, 2022, https://www.klove.com/news/faith/bible-interest-not-in-decline-youversion-bible-app-hits-an-incredible-half-billion-free-downloads-27206.

31 Billy Graham, "Why I Believe the Bible Is the Word of God," Decision Magazine, last modified May 13, 2019, accessed June 15, 2022, https://decision-magazine.com/why-i-believe-bible-word-god/.

To see God's redemptive promise of Genesis be carried through Noah, Abraham, Moses, David, and Jesus reveals the magnificent and cross-generational agreement of Scripture. In addition, when you read the Gospels you can't help but see the self-authenticating power of Christ. As C.S. Lewis once stated, "Jesus was either a liar, lunatic or Lord."[32] The claims of Jesus were radical, extreme, and history altering. In the early 1800s, the French military leader Napoleon Bonaparte once spoke of the majesty of Jesus when he said:

"Alexander, Caesar, Charlemagne and myself founded empires. But on what did we rest the creations of our genius? Upon sheer force. Jesus Christ alone founded His empire upon love; and at this hour millions of men will die for Him. In every other existence but that of Christ how many imperfections! From the first day to the last He is the same; majestic and simple; infinitely firm and infinitely gentle. He proposes to our faith a series of mysteries and commands with authority that we should believe them, giving no other reason than those tremendous words, 'I am God.' The Bible contains a complete series of acts and of historical men to explain time and eternity, such as no other religion has to offer. If it is not the true religion, one is very excusable in being deceived; for everything in it is grand and worthy of God."[33]

---

32 C.S. Lewis, Mere Christianity (New York: Simon and Schuster, 1996).

33 Eva Marshall Shonts, The World's Need? One Hundred Other Momentous Questions in History (Chicago: The Forget-me-not Pub. Co, 1920).

Now, if the Bible made several claims that were false in history, that were false in geography, that were false in archeology, and that were false in theology and anthropology and there was evidence for systemic and consistent contradictions, clashes, and inconsistencies, then you would have valid grounds to reject the reliability of the Bible. However, as we have seen, that's simply not the case. The harmony and accuracy of Scripture is abundant and overwhelming.

Biblical Reliability

As we further our journey to investigate the trustworthiness of Scripture, we must continue to confront common questions. For example, what about those who claim that Scripture has been changed or modified? In other words, how do we know that what the Apostles and Prophets wrote is the same content that we have in our Bibles today? Namely, do these accusations have any weight? Dr. Daniel Wallace, the President of the Center for the Study of New Testament Manuscripts, studies the textual consistency found within the quantity of early Greek manuscripts. He demonstrates the reliability through the uniformity of manuscripts that date back to just decades after the originals were written. For example, the earliest New Testament fragment we have is from approximately 100 A.D. (around the death of the Apostle John). The fragment was discovered in 1934 and is called P52 (for papyrus 52). It holds a portion of John 18:31–33 on one side and John 18:37–38 on the other that matches the exact text of our modern Greek New Testament. But we have much more than one fragment. In fact, Dr. Wallace says, "In comparison with the average ancient Greek author, the New Testament copies are well over a thousand times more plentiful. If the average-sized manuscript were two and one-half inches thick, all the copies of the works of an average Greek author (Plato, Aristotle, Homer, etc.) would stack up four feet high, while the copies of the New Testament would stack up to over a mile high! This is indeed an embarrassment of riches."[34]

When you add this fact to the astonishing discovery of the Dead Sea Scrolls in 1947 which include fragments from every Old Testament book (except the book of Esther), the unreliability of biblical texts becomes painfully difficult to argue. That is to say, textual critics have revealed that the biblical text in our ancient scrolls (Dead Sea Scrolls and New Testament Scrolls) is 99% identical to the text in our modern biblical manuscripts. In short, the modern Bibles are a reliable representation of the original Hebrew and Greek manuscripts. Ultimately, we have a God who does not permit His words to be lost, perverted or damaged. In the end, we can conclude that we have strong (even overwhelming) evidence that substantiates the reliability of the Bible. But more than that, we can conclude that we have accurate information about God, ourselves, and the only Gospel that saves. Michael Houdmann, summed up this point when he wrote, "We believe that the God who created the universe is capable of writing a book.

34 Justin Taylor and Daniel B. Wallace, "An Interview with Daniel B. Wallace on the New Testament Manuscripts," The Gospel Coalition, last modified March 22, 2012, accessed June 15, 2022, https://www.thegospelcoalition.org/blogs/justin-taylor/an-interview-with-daniel-b-wallace-on-the-new-testament-manuscripts/.

And the God who is perfect is capable of writing a perfect book. The issue is not simply "Does the Bible have a mistake?" but "Can God make a mistake?" If the Bible contains factual errors, then God is not omniscient and is capable of making errors Himself. If the Bible contains misinformation, then God is not truthful but is instead a liar. If the Bible contains contradictions, then God is the author of confusion. In other words, if biblical inerrancy is not true, then God is not God."[35]

The Doctrine of the Sufficiency of Scripture

Now, while we have established biblical divinity, authority, and reliability we must now look to biblical sufficiency. In other words, is the Bible we have sufficient to accomplish the mission of God? Does the church have a need for further divinely inspired words or prophetic revelation? Are we lacking truth? More precisely, are the 66 books of the Old and New Testaments all we need for righteous morality, faithful spirituality, and the establishment of God's Kingdom on earth? During the Reformation of the 16th-century, this was a forefront issue. Under Roman Catholic doctrine, Scripture alone was *not* sufficient. In fact, they still hold this position today. They claimed a requirement for a triad of Scripture, papal writings, and church tradition. Namely, they believe in papal infallibility which is a doctrine that states the Pope, when he speaks ex-cathedra (from the chair of authority),

---

35 Michael Houdmann, "Home," GotQuestions.org, last modified February 9, 2007, accessed June 15, 2022, https://www.gotquestions.org/Biblical-inerrancy.html.

is preserved from the possibility of an error in doctrine.[36] Namely, they believe in ongoing, infallible revelation. This is in stark contrast to the Protestant doctrine of *Sola Scriptura* (Latin for Scripture alone), which states the Bible is the sole, infallible, and complete source of authority for Christian faith and practice. This position is anchored in several key passages of Scripture including 2 Peter 1:3 which says, "His divine power has granted to us all things that pertain to life and godliness, through the knowledge of him who called us to his own glory and excellence…" The Westminster Confession of Faith defines the Bible this way, "The whole counsel of God, concerning all things necessary for his own glory, man's salvation, faith, and life, is either expressly set down in Scripture, or by good and necessary consequence may be deduced from Scripture: unto which nothing at any time is to be added, whether by new revelations of the Spirit, or traditions of men."[37]

As mentioned earlier, 2 Timothy 3:16–17 is another hallmark text demonstrating the sufficiency of Scripture. It states, "All Scripture is breathed out by God and profitable for teaching, for reproof, for correction, and for training in righteousness, so that the man of God may be complete, equipped for every good work." The key text begins at the purpose clause in verse 17 that says, "so that the man of God may be complete." Namely, the purpose of all Scripture being breathed out by God is to complete the man

36 "Papal Infallibility," Wikipedia (Wikimedia Foundation, May 27, 2022), last modified May 27, 2022, accessed June 15, 2022, https://en.wikipedia.org/wiki/Papal_infallibility.

37 Westminster Confession of Faith (Glasgow, Scotland: Free Presbyterian Publications, 2003).

of God. That is, humanity does not need any further information beyond holy Scripture to bring about spiritual totality, maturity, and wholeness. At the center, this teaches us that there is no higher court or content by which the church (or humanity for that matter) can appeal for truth. Psalm 19:7–10 affirms this fact when David wrote, "The law of the Lord is perfect, reviving the soul; the testimony of the Lord is sure, making wise the simple; the precepts of the Lord are right, rejoicing the heart; the commandment of the Lord is pure, enlightening the eyes; the fear of the Lord is clean, enduring forever; the rules of the Lord are true, and righteous altogether. More to be desired are they than gold, even much fine gold; sweeter also than honey and drippings of the honeycomb."

While Christ is truth in a Person, the Bible is truth in a book. All other truths must be measured against Scripture. In fact, recently the famed psychologist, Jordan Peterson (who does not profess to be a Christian) said in an interview, "It's not that the Bible is true. It's that the Bible is the prerequisite for the manifestation of truth, which makes it far more true than just 'true.' It's a whole different kind of truth. And I think that's not just literally the case—in fact—I think it can't be otherwise. This is the only way to solve the problem of perception."[38] Fascinatingly, Peterson grasps, in a sense, the sufficiency of Scripture. He understands that truth begins with God and since the Bible is God's Word, there is no greater fountain for truthful practice than the Bible.

---

38 Billy Hallowell, "Famed Psychologist Jordan Peterson Tells Joe Rogan Why the Bible Is 'Way More True than Just True'," CBN News (CBN News, January 28, 2022), last modified January 28, 2022, accessed June 15, 2022, Search at: https://www1.cbn.com/.

In fact, Colossians 2:8 actually warns Christians about turning to any other human authority other than the words of God when it says, "See to it that no one takes you captive by philosophy and empty deceit, according to human tradition, according to the elemental spirits of the world, and not according to Christ." This, as you may know, has not been a command the modern church has followed. With the all-too-common adoption of church growth techniques, churches have turned to extra-biblical means to attract and entertain crowds. As a result, this has won church attenders not to Scripture (or to Christ for that matter) but to the unsustainable and empty practices of human philosophy and tradition. It is, in a very real sense, the practice of denying the Doctrine of Sufficiency of Scripture.

Now, while Christians believe that the Bible alone is sufficient for Christian faith and practice, we are not *solo Scriptura*. That is, we are not *Scripture-only* people (in the wooden sense). Yes, the Scriptures have the ultimate and reigning authority and cannot be rivaled by any other content. But too often, in the church, we find groups which I have called "Me, My Bible, and I" Christians. These are individuals who operate independently of church history rejecting the value of orthodox confessions, creeds, and commentaries. They are "Jesus is my theology" people who fail to see the Holy Spirit's work throughout the universal church for the edification of the Body of Christ (including them). It was Charles Spurgeon who once said of these people, "It seems odd, that certain men who talk so much of what the Holy Spirit reveals to themselves, should think so little of what he has revealed to others." [39] This detachment from church history and their spiritual lineage is, in many ways, an exaggeration of the Protestant ethic *sola Scriptura*. We must remember that the Reformers stood behind and taught the Apostles' Creed, the Nicene Creed, and the Athanasian Creed. Martin Luther, John Calvin, John Knox, and the rest of the reformers leveraged theological resources, commentaries, and even catechisms. They viewed an anti-creedal and anti-confessional theology as anti-Christian. [40] Therefore, to operate as an island in church history is not an attitude supported by sola Scriptura. Scripture alone simply means that all confessions, creeds, and commentaries must remain subordinate to, and agree with, Scripture. R. C. Sproul demonstrates the balance of this position when he states:

> "Although tradition does not rule our interpretation, it does guide it. If upon reading a particular passage you have come up with an interpretation that has escaped the notice of every other Christian for two thousand years, or has been championed by universally recognized heretics, chances are pretty good that you had better abandon your interpretation." [41]

---

39 Charles Spurgeon, Commenting & Commentaries—Lecture 1, accessed June 15, 2022, https://archive.spurgeon.org/misc/c&cl1.php.

40 Jason Helopoulos, "Is Scripture Alone the Same Thing as Scripture Only?," Tabletalk, last modified July 30, 2019, accessed June 15, 2022,

41 Michael Horton, R.C. Sproul, The Agony of Deceit (Chicago, IL: Moody Press, 1990) 34-35.

That is, at this point in history, we have had nearly two millennia of theologically scrutinized, Holy Spirit illuminated, and pastorally clarified doctrine. That is to say, the Christian faith has been thoroughly codified. For example, if you are advocating for a Christianity that stands in opposition to great confessions like the Westminster Confession of Faith or the 1689 Baptist Confession of Faith, it's very likely that you are operating outside of historic, evangelical orthodoxy. Ultimately, true Protestants still value theological and historical contributions. But we only value those contributions that adhere to Scripture. These contributions are not inerrant like Scripture but they are helpful and edifying resources produced by God's providence for the edification of the church.

Conclusion

Scripture is authoritative, infallible, inspired, reliable, and sufficient. In short, the Bible has proven itself as the ultimate source of truth. However, we still have an enemy who is always looking for ways to diminish the confidence humanity has in the Word of God. He knows he doesn't have to disprove God's Word, he simply needs to birth doubt. Combine this with the fallen nature of man and you begin to see the all-out spiritual assault aiming to leave humanity divided, confused, and unsure of the authority and credibility of the Bible. I appreciate the words of the 1800s minister Henry Ward Beecher when he said, "Sink the Bible to the bottom of the ocean, and still man's obligations to God would be unchanged. He would have the same path to tread, only his lamp and guide would be gone; the same voyage to make, but his chart and compass would be overboard."[42] The Bible is a gift. God has not left us without clarity. We are not lost. He has revealed Himself to us in Scripture. Therefore, the Bible is the greatest gift of truth to touch the face of the earth.

---

42 Henry Ward Beecher, Life Thoughts: Gathered from The Extemporaneous Discourses of Henry Ward Beecher (Nabu Press, 2010), 143.

Chapter Five

HOW IS TRUTH
INTERPRETED?

———

In 512 B.C., as Darius the First of Persia led his armies north of the Black Sea, the Scythians sent him a message consisting of a mouse, a frog, a bird, and five arrows. Darius summoned his captains. "Our victory is assured," he announced. "These arrows signify that the Scythians will lay down their arms; the mouse means the land of the Scythians will be surrendered to us; the frog means that their rivers and lakes will also be ours; and the Scythian army will fly like a bird from our forces."

But an advisor to Darius said, "The Scythians mean by these things that unless you turn into birds and fly away, or into frogs and hide in the waters, or into mice and burrow for safety in the ground, you will all be slain by the Scythian archers." Darius humbly took counsel and decided his interpretation was wrong. As a result, he won the battle.[43] Ultimately, this story teaches us

---

43 Moody Bible Institute, "Today in the Word," Today in the Word, Jan. 1, 1992.

that interpretation can significantly alter the outcome of our life. Therefore, having access to truth is not sufficient. We must also have the ability to rightly interpret it.

In 2020, I remember speaking to a group of college students regarding marriage and sexuality. In my lecture, I presented the case for binary gender, traditional marriage, and heterosexuality based on Scripture. After my presentation, I had a student approach me and say, "Your talk was insightful but it's simply your interpretation." This was, of course, a common response from a culture saturated in relativism. In short, the student was aiming to reduce my interpretation of Scripture to mere opinion. But his statement raises a good question. How do we differentiate between faithful interpretation and opinion? Better yet, how do we know which interpretation is correct or flawed? To answer these questions, we must turn to the field of hermeneutics. The term *hermeneutics* is derived from the Greek noun *hermēneia* (ἑρμηνεία), which means "translation" or "interpretation." When we use the word in the singular (e.g., My hermeneutic), it refers to the set of interpretive principles a particular person holds. Historically, the Protestant Church has held to what is called the Grammatical-Historical Hermeneutic. This is a method of literal interpretation which means taking the text plainly according to both the genre and the grammatical and historical context in which the text sits. As we know, accurate interpretation, especially biblical interpretation, is no easy task. Scripture is ancient writing from a foreign land in a distant time in a foreign language. The ability to accurately grasp the figures of speech, the idioms, poetry, cultural references, local customs, geographics, and the historical understanding of the authors and recipients of these biblical writings is complex. The ultimate goal of faithfully apprehending these various aspects of interpretation is to accurately interpret meaning. But what is meaning? Who determines meaning and how can we be sure we have arrived at a truthful interpretation of meaning?

The Search for Meaning

During my years at The Master's Seminary, my hermeneutics professor Dr. Brad Klassen defined meaning as "the content of a communication, which a writer (or speaker) *consciously willed to convey* by the words (sharable symbols) and grammar (sharable structures) he used" (emphasis original).[44] In short, meaning is synonymous with authorial intent. Although hermeneutics deals with the practical methodology of interpretation (which we will discuss shortly), the first order of hermeneutical practice is to determine who has the authority to define the intent and, ultimately, the meaning of a particular text. In a time where relativism rules, much of modern culture believes that the reader is the one who determines meaning. However, this is faulty thinking. The term "author" is derived from the word "authority" because it is the author (and him alone) who has the authority to define meaning. Namely, the meaning of a text is not determined by the reader's response to the text, but by the author's intended

---

44 Dr. Brad Klassen, "The Master's Seminary," BI505 Hermeneutics Class Notes (January 6, 2017).

meaning displayed in the words they have written.

Therefore, our goal as interpreters is to unearth meaning. Notice, however, that I am using meaning in the singular. That is to say, there is only one meaning. Since there can only be one intent per text, the idea of a double meaning, historical meaning, or hidden meaning is inconsistent with logic. Therefore, the intent of the original author to the original audience is the *only* meaning that exists. Fee and Stuart explained this concept by saying, "A text cannot mean what it could never have meant for its original readers/hearers. Or to put it in a positive way, the true meaning of the biblical text for us is what God originally intended it to mean when it was first spoken or written."[45]

When speaking of Scripture, we must also breach the issue of human intent versus Divine intent. While there are various perspectives available on the participation and balance between human and Divine intent, I believe the concept of divine concursus most faithfully captures reality. The late Dr. Benjamin Warfield of Princeton Seminary once summarized this process by the following way:

"The fundamental principle of this conception is that the whole of Scripture is the product of divine activities which enter it, however, not by superseding the activities of the human authors, but confluently with them; so that the Scriptures are the joint product of divine and human activ-

---

45 Gordon D. Fee and Douglas Stuart, How to Read the Bible for All Its Worth, 4th ed. (Grand Rapids: Zondervan Publishing, 2014), 34-35.

ities, both of which penetrate them at every point, working harmoniously together to the production of a writing which is not divine here and human there, but at once divine and human in every part, every word and every particular."[46]

Ultimately, hermeneutics is a robust discipline that requires a foundation of literary, grammatical, and biblical knowledge to even begin the process of faithful interpretation. But we have not been left without a toolbox. In fact, Scripture itself reveals how Scripture should be interpreted. However, beyond that, there are further biblically-backed skills that can be learned and deployed to help average Christians read, understand, and apply the truth of Scripture to their lives.

Your Hermeneutical Toolbox

Accurate interpretation is not merely a virtue of honesty; it's biblical. While we do not have space to exposit the many passages relating to precision when it comes to studying God's Word, one passage in particular is essential. In 2 Timothy 2:15, Paul exhorts his pastoral apprentice to faithful study of Scripture. He says, "Be diligent to present yourself approved to God as a workman who does not need to be ashamed, handling accurately the word of truth." Paul calls Timothy to diligent piety through a faithful comprehension of Scripture. That is, workers of the Word cannot

---

46 Benjamin B. Warfield, "Divine and Human in the Bible," in Selected Shorter Writings of Benjamin B. Warfield, Volume 1, ed. John E. Meeter (Phillipsburg, NJ: Presbyterian & Reformed, 1970), 547.

stand before God without shame if they do not handle the Word with precision and care. D. A. Carson once said, "If you are not a student of the Word, you are not called to be a teacher of the Word."[47] James 3:1 reminds us of the increased responsibility for those who communicate the Word of God to others. He writes, "Let not many of you become teachers, my brethren, knowing that as such we will incur a stricter judgment." In short, misuse or false teaching does not go unnoticed to God. That is to say, our interpretive errors have real consequences. For that reason, how does a person arrive at an accurate interpretation of the Word of Truth? What tools are seen in Scripture? What skills are encouraged by the holy authors? But most practically, what examples and resources have the faithful Christians of church history left us to leverage?

In seminary, I learned a simple, yet powerful process for interpretation that I still use today. In fact, I use it weekly to prepare sermons, podcasts, teachings, and manuscripts for books on biblical topics. It's a five-part acronym called A.O.I.M.A., which stands for Analyzation, Observation, Interpretation, Meaning, and Application. This straightforward process enables everyday Bible readers to apply faithful hermeneutical principles that support their efforts to arrive at the true meaning of a particular biblical text. And this is the goal—rightly interpreting Scripture in an effort to arrive at the truth.

Now, each of these steps can be carried out at varying

---

47 D. A. Carson, For the Love of God: A Daily Companion for Discovering the Riches of God's Word (Nottingham: Inter-Varsity Press, 2010).

depths. At this time, I will only be offering a brief, but still useful summary of each of these five stages. If you decide to add depth to the process, these summaries will act as guides for directing those efforts. Having said that, I have taught this process enough at our school (Reformation Seminary) for long enough to know that if you don't apply these principles they won't sink in. For that reason, after you finish this book, consider employing these principles during a personal study of a short New Testament epistle. At that point you will see the rich value of this process and leverage it in personal study or in your opportunities to teach.

Note: A collection of study Bibles, commentaries, and a good biblical atlas will prove to be immensely helpful in this process.

Stage #1 Analyzation

The primary focus of this stage is to understand the broad historical and cultural context of a particular biblical book prior to studying individual chapters or verses. I carry out the following process by adding my notes from each of these steps to a nicely organized Word document. Not only does this allow me to keep a record of my biblical book studies but I can also reference them again during future study of smaller portions of these specific books. For example, if you analyze the book of John and end up with an 8–10 page Word Document overview with collected notes, links, images, and resources and then two years later you teach a Bible study on John 3, you can easily reference your analysis to be sure you are faithfully interpreting the content of your focus chapter or passage.

Read The Book Multiple Times. It often takes several readings of a biblical text to begin seeing the thematic thread and the author's general intentions. The goal of broad reading is to understand context. Context is simply the setting in which a particular book or text has been woven. Therefore, you should identify the religious context, geographic context, political context, social-economic context, and even the architectural and agricultural context. As my professor would always tell us, "It's your job to construct a mental picture of this historical world. If you don't understand the context you will never be able to accurately interpret the truth."

Study the Author of the Text. In order to eventually understand the authorial intent, you must understand the author. Essentially you need to conduct a biographical analysis. This would include answering questions like: Who is the author? When and where was he born? What is most notable about him? What else has he written?

Study the Location of the Text. Location impacts writing more than we might think. For example, much of the Bible is written to an agrarian culture who comprehended the vast number of farming metaphors, parables, and illustrations used in Scripture. For that reason, you need to know where your letter was written and where it was received. But more than that, how does geography affect the content of the text? What local customs, architecture, or land monuments were nearby? Was it a coastal town, desert, or city? Was it rural or metropolitan? These are vital contextual questions.

Study The Recipients of the Text. If the author is the root and stem then the recipients are the rose. When we understand who these people are, their need for this letter, their ethnic heritage (Greek, Jew, or both), their strengths and weaknesses, and their social setting we will have a far greater chance at accurately interpreting our biblical text.

Define The Purpose of the Correspondence. After reading and reviewing your biblical text, understanding the author, the location, and the recipients, it's time to produce a short, Roman Numeral outline of the book. Start by writing a succinct 2–5 sentence summary defining the purpose for the correspondence and then list your outline below. If you cannot, with confidence and clarity, define the purpose of the book you're studying, you are not ready to faithfully study the individual chapters, passages, or verses.

Stage #2 Observation

In shifting from the broad context of a biblical book to the specific context of a particular passage (2–10 verses), we move from analyzation to observation. Observation has been called the art of taking notice of the unnoticeable. As it pertains to

Scripture, it's an exercise in literary awareness. The purpose of this phase is not to interpret but to become intimately aware of the specific text you're studying. Remember, observing is different than seeing. In fact, Sherlock Holmes once said, "You see, but you do not observe." Observing is restricting familiarity and presumption and seeing every detail without reservation. Consider I gave you an apple and asked you to describe it for me. Your answer would likely be, "It's red, circular, spherical, and it has a stem." Now consider if I gave you an apple and asked you to make 100 observations in writing. You would drastically change your approach from seeing to observing. You begin to notice the blemishes, the thickness of the skin, the fibrous matter on the inside, and the organic shape. Next, you would cut the apple open and see the growth lines, the seed cavities, and the seeds. But more than that, you would describe these seeds and their interiors, the growth model from seedling to seed-bearing fruit, and you would even explain the stem's relationship to the weight of the apple. This is observation and it's an essential part of faithful interpretation. Now, it's important to state that observation is not interpretation. Work to restrain yourself from interpreting until you have all the information to do it well. In relation to Scripture, observation is carried out in four ways.

1. **Grammar:** Words combined together become the vehicle to meaning. Therefore, observing words becomes essential. While understanding the eight parts of speech is helpful, you must also be able to identify subjects, objects, indirect

objects, coordinating conjunctions, pronouns and their antecedents, participles, infinitives (to + verb), imperatives, tense (past, present, future), main clauses (subject and verb), prepositional phrases, developing clauses (contrast clauses, purpose clauses, result clauses, contingency clauses, causal clauses, concessive clauses, temporal clauses, relative clauses, and sequential clauses). I know… You're probably panicking after that sentence. For most people, this can be an overwhelming task. For that reason, I do offer a short video covering biblical grammar and block diagramming that you can purchase at Relearn.org/Diagram. That said, we must remember that Scripture is literature and you cannot rightly observe literature without a strong grasp of basic grammar. I will make a quick reference to the value of learning biblical Greek and Hebrew. This is not a task for every Christian but it certainly and dramatically increases your ability to accurately interpret God's Word.

2. **Mood.** During your observation pay attention not only to what was said but also to how it was said. Is the text corrective, instructive, gentle, encouraging, exhorting, rebuking, harsh, explanatory, warning, condemning, etc.? By identifying mood in your text you will be able to understand the emotional context in which it was written and how it was received.

3. **Genre.** The Bible offers eight generally accepted literary genres: law, narrative, history, wisdom and poetry, prophetic,

gospel, epistle, and apocalyptic. In each of these genres we see a variety of figures of speech that are important to identify (simile, metaphor, hyperbole, irony, euphemism, personification, etc.). By identifying the genre of the biblical book you are interpreting, you will be more equipped to make correct observations about the text.

4. **Block Diagramming.** A block diagram is a method of observation that allows a reader to visually see the literary structure of a particular text (generally 2–10 verses at a time). Essentially, it's a process that allows you to see the grammatical units of your particular passage in blocks or groups. You begin by placing your passage in a Word document. Generally speaking, every English sentence has one main clause (subject + verb). These main clauses remain left-aligned in your document and the dependent clauses or modifying clauses (which are generally identified as prepositional phrases) are placed beneath them. Ultimately, the main value of block diagramming is the ability to see the central points of a text that, when in paragraph form, are difficult to recognize. Below I have offered a short example diagram of Ephesians 2:1–2. I have underlined the main clause and placed the portions of the passage that modify the main clause appropriately beneath.

Block Diagram of Ephesians 2:1–3

1 And

<u>you were dead</u>

      in the trespasses

      and

      sins in which you once walked,

      following the course

            of this world,

      following the prince

            of the power

            of the air,

            the spirit that is now at work

                   in the sons of disobedience

Ultimately, block diagramming allows the reader to have an intimate relationship with the grammar of a particular biblical text. It allows the interpreter to see literary patterns, structures, clauses, lists, and connections that are lost in text format. After all, Jesus says in Matthew 5:18, "For truly, I say to you, until heaven and earth pass away, not an iota, not a dot, will pass from the Law until all is accomplished." In other words, God is meticulous. Every word and punctuation matters to Him. Therefore, we must study and observe with precision.

Note: Block Diagramming is a very effective tool for didactic texts like the epistles but it proves to be far more difficult to apply to narrative and poetic texts like 1 Samuel, portions of the Gospels, or the Psalms. That said, narrative and poetry genres require the reader to look beyond grammatical symmetry and into the changing of scenes, character development, and plot development.

Stage #3 Interpretation

Psalm 119:34 reminds us of why we work so diligently to interpret accurately. David (the most likely author) says, "Give me understanding, that I may keep your law and observe it with my whole heart." Our aim in seeking truthful understanding of God is that we may observe God's law (for those in the New Covenant—the law of faith and the Moral Law of Sinai) and observe God's ways with our whole heart. Namely, our process for analyzation and observation is to understand (by way of interpretation) the author's intended meaning (via divine and human concursus). One theologian said, "Interpretation is, in effect, the act of recreating in one's own mind the author's willfully expressed thoughts."[48] Roy Zuck in his book Biblical Interpretation describes the differences between observation and interpretation when he wrote, "In observing what the Bible says, you probe; in interpretation, you mull. Observation is discovery; interpreting is digesting. Observation means depicting what is there, and interpretation is deciding what it means. One is to

---

48 Dr. Brad Klassen, "The Master's Seminary," BI505 Hermeneutics Class Notes (January 6, 2017).

explore, the other is to explain."[49]

Interpretation is taking the pieces you have collected during the first two phases, working them through further analysis (a.k.a exegesis). It's recognizing the difference between texts that are descriptive and texts that are prescriptive. It's word studies in the original languages, theological analysis, reviewing clauses, and drawing conclusions that are both congruent with the canon of Scripture and the consistent conclusions of historical orthodox Christianity. Now, as a side note, this doesn't mean that church history determines biblical interpretation. But it does mean that, after 2,000 years of Christian history, you are extremely unlikely to arrive at an interpretation that has been overlooked by the many generations of faithful, Holy Spirit-indwelt believers. In the end, interpreters must be chained to the text. They are faithfully, carefully, and prayerfully attempting to arrive at the right interpretation that they may rightly know God, obey God, serve God, and teach others about God.

Stage #4 Meaning

In the same way that analyzation and observation are condensed into interpretation, interpretation is condensed to meaning. While the interpretation can be robust and theological, the meaning is succinct and practical. Furthermore, it's important to clarify that the process of identifying meaning is specifically for passages of Scripture and not chapters or books. As mentioned

---

49 Roy B. Zuck, Basic Bible Interpretation (Colorado Springs, Co.: Chariot Victor Pub., 1991), 12.

earlier, there is one meaning per coherent biblical thought. The academic term for one, coherent thought in Scripture is *pericope*. A pericope is generally the number of verses used in an expository sermon (2–10 is common unless you're in a narrative text which may be longer). Therefore, the task of this stage is simple: In one sentence, take your interpretation of your pericope and identify the author's intended meaning for the original audience in the most exact, memorable sentence possible.

The author of *Biblical Preaching*, Haddon Robinson once said, "I have a conviction that no sermon is ready for preaching, not ready for writing out, until we can express its theme in a short, pregnant sentence as clear as a crystal."[50] Again, meaning is the product of interpretation but its aim is application. Namely, the meaning is the practical, everyday summation of your biblical text. It is the consolidated and compressed truth squeezed from the text and ready to be consumed. This process of boiling down and arriving at a crisp meaning of the text takes time. In fact, it can be even painful. But it's worth it. It's worth taking everything you have learned and summing it up in a consumable and dispensable statement of truth. This process done over and over and over again is the architecture for doctrinal development and ultimately systematic theology (the focus of the following chapter). When an interpreter has arrived at a clear understanding of countless passages of Scripture, they are beginning to see the skeleton of God. They are, in a very real sense, able to

---

50 Haddon Robinson, Biblical Preaching (Ada, MI: Baker Academic, 1980), 23.

understand the web of biblical theology, the interdependence of Scripture, the glory of the Gospel, and the majesty of God.

Stage #5 Application

Unearthing the meaning of Scripture may be the goal of interpretation, but it is not the end. The end is application. As we know, Hebrews 4:12 tells us that the Word of God is "living" and "active." For that reason, we must not treat the truth of God's Word merely as knowledge to apprehend but wisdom to apply. Essentially, we must conform our lives to the meaning we have uncovered. Application involves relating the unchanging meaning of the ancient text to the life of the contemporary reader.[51]

Interestingly, while there is only one meaning of a particular text there are multiple applications. Having said that, application is still handcuffed to meaning. Namely, you cannot expect to apply the meaning of a Scripture in an area outside of the jurisdiction of its meaning. For example, we cannot apply the meaning of Ephesians 5:22–33 (which is on marriage representing Christ and the church) to how we should relate to one another in business or parenting. In other words, application, while different from meaning, is controlled by meaning. J. I. Packer once said, "a ministry which is wholly concerned with gospel truths can still go wrong by giving those truths an inaccurate application. Scripture is full of truth that will heal souls,

---

51 Dr. Brad Klassen, "The Master's Seminary," BI505 Hermeneutics Class Notes (January 6, 2017).

just as a pharmacy is stocked with remedies for bodily disorders; but in both cases a misapplication of what, rightly used, will heal, will have a disastrous effect."[52]

Ultimately, application is the climax of hermeneutics. It takes academia and turns it into worship and devotion. But even more than that, it's obedience. The Apostle James reminds us, in 1:22–25, "But prove yourselves doers of the word, and not merely hearers who delude themselves. For if anyone is a hearer of the word and not a doer, he is like a man who looks at his natural face in a mirror; for once he has looked at himself and gone away, he has immediately forgotten what kind of person he was. But one who looks intently at the perfect law, the law of liberty, and abides by it, not having become a forgetful hearer but an effectual doer, this man will be blessed in what he does."

Conclusion

Interpreting truth is essential. A misinterpreted Bible is a misunderstood Bible. A misunderstood Bible is a misapplied Bible. A misapplied Bible leaves people confused and broken. Therefore, every Christian should hold to sound hermeneutics. It is these principles that permit us to form the ground of good theology. With a firm foundation in place we can begin to build upon it. We can begin to see the different facets of God's character and how they form a mountain of majesty. It is from this place of sound doctrine layered upon further sound doctrine that begins

---

52 J. I. Packer, "Give Me Understanding," in Truth and Power, 244.

to open our eyes to the greatness of our God. From here we get to put together the larger picture of God. Like laying down to look up at Michelangelo's work in the Sistine Chapel, we get to gaze upon God's beauty through sound systematic theology.

Chapter Six

WHAT IS SYSTEMATIC
THEOLOGY?

———

WHAT IS SYSTEMATIC THEOLOGY?

Humans love systems. We love them because they allow our minds to organize large volumes of content for greater understanding. When we can organize data and classify it, our minds are able to see the relationships between two or more points. On the other hand, without systems our minds become overwhelmed with the data, and the relationships between points become unclear. In short, systems help us grasp more with less effort.

Similarly to systems, humans love patterns. Patterns provide a sense of order in what might otherwise appear chaotic. Scripture tells us that God is a God of order (1 Cor 14:33). We see this in the Trinity, the human body, the seasons, and even the Scriptures. As humans, God designed our minds to see patterns. We, like God, love order. In fact, cognitive scientists at the University of Rochester explain why order matters when the human mind processes information. Professor Richard Aslin explained, "[Order is] a part of the natural statistics of the real world, and therefore a signal—or cue—that can be the basis of rational decisions."[53] Professor Aslin simply revealed what Christians already know—humans are made in the image of an orderly God. For this reason, humans love a systematic approach to most things—including theology. But loving something does not make that something easy. Systematic theology is still a rigorous discipline. However, when the teachings of the Bible are systematized and organized into an orderly and palatable pattern of information, the Christian mind rejoices! Ultimately, it's worth the effort to see God more clearly.

The goal of this chapter (and this book for that matter) is to offer you a basic understanding of systematic theology to set the stage for further study. Think of previous chapters as the foundation and this chapter as the frame from which you can build upon. Now, the question of this chapter is simple: What is systematic theology? Webster defines it as: "A form of theology in which the aim is to arrange religious truths in a self-consistent whole." Joel Beeke, President of Puritan Reformed Seminary, speaks of it this way, "Systematic theology allows near-sighted sinners with a pair of lenses through which to see God's glory in all of life."[54] R.C. Sproul defined it this way:

---

53 Peter Iglinski, "Researchers Explain How Our Minds Make Sense through Order," NewsCenter, last modified December 29, 2014, accessed June 15, 2022, https://www.rochester.edu/newscenter/making-sense-through-order-83092/.

54 Why We Need Systematic Theology, YouTube (Crossway, 2018), accessed June 15, 2022, https://www.youtube.com/watch?v=yh3FHQ7o8G0.

"Systematic theology is theology that is systematic. It is the study of the things of God in a systematic, orderly fashion, where we not only consider what this text says or that text says, but where we consider all that the Word says about something like revelation, then all the Word tells us about who God is, then all that the Word tells us about who Jesus is, and then all that the Word says about what God has done for us. Systematic theology then goes on to consider other doctrines like: the doctrine of man, of sin, of sanctification, of the sacraments, the church and the end times. Systematic theology is a way of looking at God's revelation that strongly affirms the coherency and consistency of all that God reveals in Scripture. It is an attempt to put all texts in their ultimate context—with all other texts."[55]

All that said, systematic theology is essentially the discipline of collecting everything Scripture says on a particular biblical doctrine and harmonizing it with the other collections of biblical doctrines. It's the process of constructing a theological system consisting of essential truths that have been accurately interpreted and correspond to one another without contradiction. As I mentioned in chapter one, historically, systematic theology includes a total of ten doctrinal areas including Angelology (the study of angels), anthropology (the study of the nature of humanity), bibliology (the study of the Bible), Christology (the study of Christ), ecclesiology (the study of the church), escha-

---

55 R. C. Sproul Jr., Almighty over All: Understanding the Sovereignty of God (Grand Rapids, MI: Baker Books, 1999).

tology (the study of the end times), hamartiology (the study of sin), pneumatology (the study of the Holy Spirit), soteriology (the study of salvation), and theology proper (the study of the character of God). For example, Calvinism (a.k.a. The Doctrines of Grace) is a systematic theology of soteriology (the study of salvation). But you cannot build the soteriological doctrines of Calvinism without synchronizing them with doctrines of anthropology, Christology, and the sovereignty of God (which is part of theology proper). In other words, systematic theology is an interdependent system much like a web. That is, there are parts but only as much as the parts make up the whole.

Why You Must Become a Systematic Theologian

Many years ago, I found myself in a church with a legalistic pastor who abhorred systematic theology. To him, systematic theology was to make the natural unnatural. It was to try to put God in a box for observation. He believed that the Holy Spirit would reveal any truth of Scripture that was required for the believer in the plain reading of the text. At face value, this statement sounds noble. However, over time, it became painfully apparent that his theology looked more like Swiss Cheese than an orderly and consistent view of God. I would regularly find contradictions, incongruity, and oxymorons in his teaching.

Furthermore, we must remember that God has given the church offices of theological authority and influence to help His people form a correct, consistent, and robust view of Himself. Ephesians 4:11-14 says (emphasis added), "And He gave the apostles, the prophets, the evangelists, the shepherds and teachers, *to equip the saints for the work of ministry, for building up the body of Christ*, until we all attain to the unity of the faith and of the knowledge of the Son of God, to *mature manhood*, to the measure of the stature of the fullness of Christ, *so that we may no longer be children, tossed to and fro by the waves and carried about by every wind of doctrine*, by human cunning, by craftiness in deceitful schemes." Namely, God understands our carnal necessity for thorough instruction in order to grasp the complexities of His character, Gospel, and glory.

Another point worth noting pertains to the issue of theological oneness (1 Cor. 1:10; Titus 1:9). You must see that theological clarity produces ecclesiastical unity. Contrarily, theological ambiguity produces ecclesiastical diversity. Namely, without a systematic comprehension of God's character and Gospel, you may achieve superficial unity based on surface-level relationship, but not genuine, truth-forged unity based on essential doctrines of the faith. You may worship in the same church, but you do so in a room filled with people who each hold wildly different views about highly important matters in Scripture. This is not good. I recently saw pastor Sylvester Faravadya tweet a similar sentiment, "A church becomes a mere social club when fellowship is valued above sound doctrine." Now, you might be thinking, "So, is systematic theology divisive?" To that, I will say what I once heard John MacArthur say in a lecture at Seminary, "Yes. Theology is divisive. It divides truth from error." Having said that, our aim is not to be divisive but to be more truly unified.

Furthermore, we must be careful not to divide over non-divisive issues. That is to say, we can achieve unity without obtaining uniformity. But my central point is this, remaining in the dark, unstudied, and unable to recognize what you and other Christians truly believe is not an option. We cannot protect the truth if the truth is not clearly understood.

By God's providence and grace in His church, there has been a development of several tools to bring about a systematic understanding of God and His Gospel. The first is the historic Confessions. From the Apostles' and Nicene Creeds to the creed of Athanasius to the rich and robust treatments found in the Westminster Confession and 1689 Confession of Faith. These are rich resources of theological clarity. In fact, I recommend every Christian read these five confessions as a foundational effort to establish their own systematic theology (you can order a copy of the 1689 in modern English at Relearn.org/1689).

The second tool that has proven to be tremendously useful to me is reading the systematic theologies of other Christian scholars. I will list four in order of accessibility for the average Christian. However, I would like to note that my promotion of these books does not mean I affirm the positions of each author. While each of these men holds to sound biblical orthodoxy pertaining to the Gospel, there are differences in secondary and tertiary doctrinal positions among these theologians. For that reason, you will need to read them on your own, form your own conclusions, and determine where you land.

1. *Everyone's a Theologian: An Introduction to Systematic Theology* by R.C. Sproul (357 pages).
2. *Systematic Theology: An Introduction to Christian Belief* by John

Frame (1280 pages).

3. *Biblical Doctrine: A Systematic Summary of Bible Truth* by John MacArthur (1024 pages).

4. *Systematic Theology* by Louis Berkhof (992 pages).

Ultimately, I think of the words of Christ in His high priestly prayer in John 17, which says, "I do not ask for these only [the Apostles], but also for those who will believe in me through their word, that they may all be one, just as you, Father, are in me, and I in you, that they also may be in us, so that the world may believe that you have sent me." In other words, our ecclesiastical unity is the means by which the world will believe that God sent the Messiah. That is, our theological clarity and, ultimately, our ability to navigate and establish unity around the biblical and orthodox view of God and His Gospel become an evangelistic mark of the church. So yes, understand God. Unify with those who hold to Gospel orthodoxy. Teach those who believe wrong and be willing to love and respect those who land differently on non-essential issues.

The Sister of Systematic Theology

The study of theology is like two roads that lead to the same destination. That is, there's an alternative path to study theology. Namely, a counterpart to systematic theology. That path is called biblical theology. While systematic theology aims to collect every passage that contributes to a particular doctrine in order to present congruence with other doctrines, biblical theology aims to understand doctrines chronologically as they are revealed in

Scripture over time. Geerhardus Vos once said, "Biblical theology studies the Bible with a focus on its history, whereas systematic theology studies the Bible with a focus on doctrine."[56] Therefore, a worthy synonym to biblical theology would be "redemptive history." Namely, it is the study of God's redemptive narrative from Genesis to Revelation (in that order). Furthermore, biblical theology is constrained to the exact language of Scripture. For example, in Systematic theology you can arrive at doctrines with extra-biblical names (e.g., Trinity, Soteriology, Calvinism, Credo-baptist, Sublapsarianism, Postmillennialism, etc.) where in biblical theology you are examining the historical record of Bible-specific themes (e.g., atonement, sacrifice, sanctification, love, marriage, and sin). In addition to themes, biblical theology can also be carried out by books or corpus (all the books by one author). That is to say, while doing biblical theology you may want to see John's perspective on sin or love by reading his complete corpus. Again, this is different from systematic theology which would never restrict its study of sin to a particular time or author. No, systematic theology presents everything the Bible says about sin and how it harmonizes with other overlapping and related doctrines.

Ultimately, in systematic theology you would ask, "What does the whole Bible say about sin?" In biblical theology you would ask, "How did our understanding of sin develop over biblical history?" Therefore, biblical theology takes into account the context and information available to those at the time of its

---

56 Geerhardus Vos, Reformed Dogmatics (Bellingham, WA: Lexham Press, 2020).

revelation. In a very real way, it offers modern Christians a reason to be grateful because, unlike the saints of the past, we have the full revelation of God—from the Messiah and the cross to the promise of a second coming of Christ and the finalized canon of Scripture. So if you're fascinated with history you might lean toward the disciplines of biblical theology, but if you're a big picture visionary type (like myself) you will likely lean toward systematic theology. Both are valuable approaches to theology and, as I said, arrive at the same destination.

Chapter Seven

CONCLUSION: THE GROUND OF GOOD THEOLOGY

———

B ut why write an entire book to prepare a person to do systematic theology? Better yet, why is systematic theology important? What's the purpose of such a complex study? I have summed it up in a simple phrase: The heart cannot exult what the mind does not understand.

I remember sitting at Grace Community Church where John MacArthur once preached something similar. He said, "Our doxology (praise) can only be as high as our theology is deep." I believe this is why the Lord has included mental worship in the first and greatest commandment. Which is, as you know, "You shall love the Lord your God with all your heart and with all your soul and with all *your mind.*" (Matt 22:37). Loving God with our minds has become an almost absent practice in the modern church. We have opted for emotion and social actions but have left our intellectual worship on the sidelines. Sure, we must realize that intellectual study of theology should not remain only in the mind. These truths must translate from the head to the heart and hands. Namely, systematic theology should make us more like

Christ. It should cause our worship and praise to be magnified. It should cause us to be more humble, more compassionate, and ultimately, more like our Lord.

But more than that, systematic theology is a rigorous pursuit of coherence and defense. Let me explain. You cannot defend something that is illogical. You cannot rationalize that which is irrational. But God and the Gospel are both logical and rational. However, you cannot defend what you do not understand. Unfortunately, many Christians (if not most) are simply untrained, unstudied, and unprepared to live out and speak up, the truths of sound doctrine. For that reason, we must be willing to apply ourselves to theological rigor. To see the cohesive majesty of our God. But again this is not for academia's sake but for God-glorifying, Gospel-centered intellectual worship. In fact, in Jeremiah 9:23–24, it's this properly directed, intellectual pursuit of God that our efforts should be focused. It is, truthfully, the only time God permits us to boast. The prophet writes, "Thus says the Lord: "Let not the wise man boast in his wisdom, let not the mighty man boast in his might, let not the rich man boast in his riches, but let him who boasts boast in this, that he understands and knows me, that I am the Lord who practices steadfast love, justice, and righteousness in the earth. For in these things I delight, declares the Lord." Right knowledge of God is vital for right worship of God. Without a doubt, this is the purpose of human life. It was Jesus, in His high priestly prayer of John 17 who summed up this truth when He said, "And this is eternal life, that they know you, the only true God, and Jesus Christ whom you have sent" (John

17:3). The simplest creed of the Christian life is "Know God and make Him known." Systematic theology is merely the means by which you can achieve this knowledge. It is the method to right understanding, right worship, and ultimately, right relationship with God.

In the end, if you believe wrong, you'll never live strong. Namely, what we believe matters. Unfortunately, deception is real and the human heart is sick (Jer 17:9). We live in an emotionalized culture and we're prone to make conclusions based on feelings rather than facts. That's why writing this book was so important to me. I wanted to offer you the tools and information to define truth, find truth, know truth, and rightly interpret truth. In 1 Timothy 3:15 Paul tells the local church, "I write so that you may know how you ought to conduct yourself in the house of God, which is the church of the living God, the pillar and ground of the truth." The church is the pillar and ground of the truth in this world. Collectively, by the power of the Holy Spirit, we are the beholders and representatives of God who uphold the truth of God in this fallen world. Namely, God has entrusted us—the church with the revelation of Himself, the Gospel, and the Moral Law. Therefore, we have a duty and responsibility to be faithful with what we have been given—to study to show ourselves approved—to be diligent and careful with how we think, read, study, teach, and worship. It is here that we maintain our role as the buttress of truth. It is here that we can defend against lies and heresies and attacks. It is here that we can fulfill the Great Commission and the proclamation of God's saving grace. But most of all it is here where we can find rest for our souls. As I mentioned earlier, it was Augustine who said, "Where I found truth, there found I my God, who is the truth itself."[1] Therefore, truth and God are one. Therefore, truth is the ground. It's where we must begin and where our only hope remains. When we move from truth, we lose everything.

---

1 Augustine and Henry Bettenson, The City of God (London, England: Penguin Books, 2003).

Bibliography

CITED
MATERIALS

———

BIBLIOGRAPHY

Ardavanis, Jonny. "| John MacArthur Ep. 6." Spotify. Jonny
      Ardavanis, n.d. Accessed June 15, 2022. https://open.
      spotify.com/show/3zRD4xDc5spuY1NVeL
      wVY0?si=a7cb3a0de3704406.

Augustine, and Henry Bettenson. The City of God. London,
      England: Penguin Books, 2003.

Bannerman, James. Inspiration: The Infallible Truth and
      Divine Authority of the Holy Scriptures. Edinburgh:
      T. and T. Clark, 1865.

Beecher, Henry Ward. Life Thoughts: Gathered from The
      Extemporaneous Discourses of Henry Ward Beecher.
      Nabu Press, 2010.

Billings, Lee. "Atheism Is Inconsistent with the Scientific
      Method, Prizewinning Physicist Says." Scien
      tific American. Scientific American, March 20,
      2019. Last modified March 20, 2019. Accessed June

15, 2022. https://www.scientificamerican.com/article/
atheism-is-inconsistent-with-the-scientific-meth
od-prizewinning-physicist-says/.

Boothe, Charles Octavius. Plain Theology for Plain People.
S.l.: Albatros Publishers, 2020.

Calvin, Jean. Institutes of the Christian Religion. London:
James Clarke & Co, 1962.

Carson, D. A. For the Love of God: A Daily Companion
for Discovering the Riches of God's Word.
Nottingham: Inter-Varsity Press, 2010.

Charnock, Stephen. Discourses upon the Existence and Attri
butes of God. Grand Rapids: Baker Book House,
1979.

"Correspondence Theory of Truth." Wikipedia. Wikimedia
Foundation, May 23, 2022. Last modified May 23,
2022. Accessed June 15, 2022. https://en.m.wikipedia.
org/wiki/Correspondence_theory_of_truth.

Gill, John. Gill's Commentary. Grand Rapids: Baker Book
House, 1980.

Gootjes, Nicolaas Hendrik. The Belgic Confession: Its History and Sources. Grand Rapids, MI: Baker Academic, 2007.

Graham, Billy. "Why I Believe the Bible Is the Word of God." Decision Magazine. Last modified May 13, 2019. Accessed June 15, 2022. https://decisionmagazine. com/why-i-believe-bible-word-god/.

Hallowell, Billy. "Famed Psychologist Jordan Peterson Tells Joe Rogan Why the Bible Is 'Way More True than Just True'." CBN News. CBN News, January 28, 2022. Last modified January 28, 2022. Accessed June 15, 2022. https://www1.cbn.com/cbnnews/ entertainment/2022/january/famed-psychologist-jordan-peterson-tells-joe-rogan-why-the-bible-is-lsquo-way-more-true-than-just-true-rsquo.

Helopoulos, Jason. "Is Scripture Alone the Same Thing as Scripture Only?" Tabletalk. Last modified July 30, 2019. Accessed June 15, 2022. https://tabletalkmag azine.com/posts/is-scripture-alone-the-same-thing-as-scripture-only/.

Hooper, Carol-Ann, and Una McCluskey. Psychodynamic Perspectives on Abuse: The Cost of Fear. London: Jessica Kingsley Publishers, 2000.

Horton, Michael, Sproul, R.C. The Agony of Deceit. Chicago, IL: Moody Press, 1990.

Houdmann, Michael. "Home." GotQuestions.org. Last modi fied February 9, 2007. Accessed June 15, 2022. https://www.gotquestions.org/Biblical-inerrancy. html.

Hunt, Richard D. "Bible Interest Not in Decline: Youversion Bible App Hits an Incredible Half-Billion Free Downloads." LOVE. Accessed June 15, 2022. https://www.klove.com/news/faith/bible-interest not-in-decline-youversion-bible-app-hits-an-i credible-half-billion-free-downloads-27206.

Iglinski, Peter. "Researchers Explain How Our Minds Make Sense through Order." NewsCenter. Last modi- fied December 29, 2014. Accessed June 15, 2022. https://www.rochester.edu/newscenter/making- sense-through-order-83092/.

Kempis, Thomas. The Imitation of Christ. New York: Dorset Press, 1952.

Klassen, Brad. "The Master's Seminary ." BI505 Hermeneu tics Class Notes (January 6, 2017).

Lawson, Steven. "What Is Truth? ." Ligonier Ministries.
Accessed June 15, 2022. https://www.ligonier.org/
learn/articles/what-is-truth.

MacArthur, John F. "Is the Bible Reliable?" Grace to You.
Last modified August 18, 2016. Accessed June 15,
2022. https://www.gty.org/library/topical-series-li
brary/65/is-the-bible-reliable.

Magazine, Smithsonian. "Evidence for a Flood." Smith
sonian.com. Smithsonian Institution, April 1, 2000.
Last modified April 1, 2000. Accessed June 15, 2022.
https://www.smithsonianmag.com/science-nature/
evidence-for-a-flood-102813115/.

Moody Bible Institute. Today in the Word, January 1, 1992.

Nickel, James. Mathematics:: Is God Silent? Vallecito, CA:
Ross House Books, 2012.

Novak, Michael. Awakening from Nihilism: Why Truth
Matters. London: IEA Health and Welfare Unit,
1995.

"Papal Infallibility." Wikipedia. Wikimedia Foundation, May
27, 2022. Last modified May 27, 2022. Accessed
June 15, 2022. https://en.wikipedia.org/wiki/Papal_

infallibility.

Rushdooney, R.J. Systematic Theology. Vallecito, California: Ross House Books, 2000.

Shonts, Eva Marshall. The World's Need? One Hundred Other Momentous Questions in History. Chicago: The Forget-me-not Pub. Co, 1920.

Sproul, R. C. Almighty over All: Understanding the Sovereignty of God. Grand Rapids, MI: Baker Books, 1999.

Sproul, R. C. Reason to Believe: A Response to Common Objections to Christianity. Grand Rapids, MI: Zondervan Pub. House, 1993.

Sproul, R.C. "One in Essence, Three in Person: Reformed Bible Studies & Devotionals at Ligonier.org: Reformed Bible Studies & Devotionals at Ligonier org." Ligonier Ministries. Accessed June 15, 2022. https://www.ligonier.org/learn/devotionals/one-essence-three-person.

Sproul, R.C. "What Is Sound Doctrine?" Ligonier Ministries. Accessed June 15, 2022. https://www.ligonier.org/learn/articles/what-sound-doctrine/.

Spurgeon , Charles. Commenting & Commentaries—
    Lecture 1. Accessed June 15, 2022. https://archive.
    spurgeon.org/misc/c&cl1.php.

Lewis, C.S.. Mere Christianity. New York: Simon and
    Schuster, 1996.

Taylor, Justin, and Daniel B. Wallace. "An Interview with
    Daniel B. Wallace on the New Testament Manu
    scripts." The Gospel Coalition. Last modified March
    22, 2012. Accessed June 15, 2022. https://www.
    thegospelcoalition.org/blogs/justin-taylor/an-inter
    view-with-daniel-b-wallace-on-the-new-testament
    manuscripts/.

Tozer, A. W. The Knowledge of the Holy: The Attributes of
    God, Their Meaning in the Christian Life. United
    States: GENERAL PRESS, 2019.

Vos, Geerhardus. Reformed Dogmatics. Bellingham, WA:
    Lexham Press, 2020.

Westminster Confession of Faith. Glasgow, Scotland: Free
    Presbyterian Publications, 2003.

"The Westminster Larger Catechism." Ligonier Ministries.
    Accessed June 15, 2022. https://www.ligonier.org/

learn/articles/westminster-larger-catechism.

Why We Need Systematic Theology. YouTube. Crossway,
2018. Accessed June 15, 2022. https://www.youtube.
com/watch?v=yh3FHQ7o8G0.

Wilson, Greg. "The Doctrine of God." I. Accessed June 15,
2022. https://libcfl.com/articles/cole-1.htm#intro.

Zuck, Roy B. Basic Bible Interpretation. Colorado Springs,
Co.: ChariotVictor Pub., 1991.

Shop.Relearn.org

OTHER TITLES BY DALE PARTRIDGE

———

LEARN BIBLICAL
MANHOOD

———

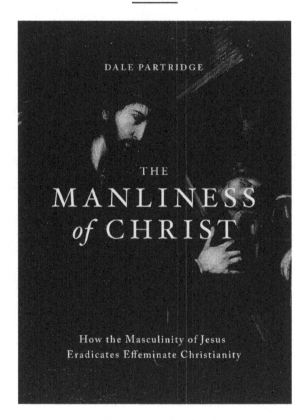

DALE PARTRIDGE

THE
MANLINESS
of CHRIST

How the Masculinity of Jesus
Eradicates Effeminate Christianity

Relearn.org/Man

LEARN ABOUT BIBLICAL HOUSE CHURCH

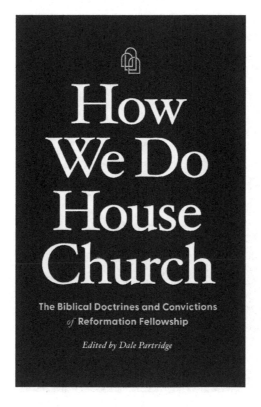

Shop.Relearn.org

READ THE
1689 CONFESSION

———

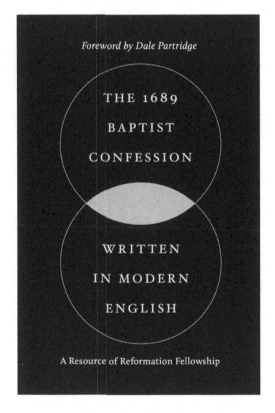

Foreword by Dale Partridge

THE 1689

BAPTIST

CONFESSION

WRITTEN

IN MODERN

ENGLISH

A Resource of Reformation Fellowship

Shop.Relearn.org

READ THE
GOSPEL

———

A Simple Presentation of

THE
GOSPEL

A MESSAGE
of LOVE

FINDING FORGIVENESS, FREEDOM, & FAMILY

MailtheGospel.org

Made in the USA
Las Vegas, NV
09 December 2022

61618269R00072